What God Has Done

What God Has Done

Inspirational Messages for Daily Living

BOB IVORY

Cover design: Cedric Sims
Editor: M. B. White
Copyright © 2015 Bob Ivory

ISBN-13: 9780692403631
ISBN-10: 0692403639
Library of Congress Control Number: 2015905474
Robert Ivory, North Randall, OH

Acknowledgments

$\mathcal{T}$here have been so many people who have inspired, supported, encouraged, and motivated me over the years that it would be impossible to name them all. I would like, however, to dedicate *What God Has Done* to my dear sister Marjie, the loving memory of my younger brother Clinton Hall Jr., and my grandparents, the late Reverend Wallis Sr. and Daisy Ivory, who adopted and raised me *and* provided me with a firm foundation. I would also like to acknowledge my dear friend Yvonne Pointer in Cleveland, Ohio, who has been an inspiration to me over the years and encouraged me years ago to write down my thoughts in book form. I also dedicate this book to the Reverend Dr. Amos C. Brown and his lovely wife, First Lady Jane Brown, and Rev. Aubrey Lewis and his lovely wife, Deacon Viola Lewis, who mentored me and were my extended family, showing me much love while I lived in the San Francisco Bay Area; to Coach Ted Ginn Sr. and former Ohio Senator C. J. Prentiss for being mentors and friends and for lighting a torch in me professionally as it relates to servicing underserved youth in the effort to help close the achievement gap and increase the high school graduation rate; to my long-time friends since college Ron Woodson, Aurelia Gamble and Sandy Mills; Rev. Dr. Marvin McMickle for his wisdom and family support; to Aimee Brountie and to my darling children, who I love endlessly: Timothy, Kyerra, Christopher, Jasmine, and Robert Jr., and my grandsons Chase and Parris, I am so very proud of each of you.

With that said, I am pleased to acknowledge and make no concessions that my ultimate inspiration comes from God Himself through His infinite wisdom, grace, goodness, mercy, and perfect will. I give Him all praise and glory as I am so thankful for all He has seen me through and has done for me. He never fails. He continues to work with and on me and all my shortcomings and imperfections. In the sweet and matchless name of my Lord and Savior Jesus Christ, I pray that throughout each day and within the pages of this book, the words from my mouth and meditation of my heart are acceptable in His sight, O Lord, my strength and my redeemer.

Contents

Introduction

*J*ust when you've come to the conclusion that you have acquired all the right combinations and ingredients for successful living, you may find yourself in search and in need of words that inspire. Words and references that edify you, motivate you, encourage you, and are relevant to your life's journey and speak to your inner being, are necessary. We all benefit at some time or another from inspiration that not only enables us to move forward on a productive, effective, and fulfilling path but also helps us to walk in our true purpose, ordered steps, and earthly assignments. I am so thankful that with all the complexities and nuances of life, the world, in most instances, is not just cut and dry, black or white, up or down, this or that. I am sure you agree that life has many dimensions and levels of awareness and consciousness to reach and attain. There remains an ever-evolving cycle of situations, circumstances, and scenarios in which our efforts and aspirations are all enhanced by one invaluable, intangible element: *inspiration.*

It is quite possible to possess all the basic tools, knowledge, skill sets, and abilities for success and yet be void of inspiration, motivation, passion, *compassion*, conviction, resolve, and purpose. Therefore, total happiness and fulfillment may appear to be out of reach. Be it an artist who approaches a blank canvas before creating a masterpiece, a songwriter with pen, paper, or instrument in hand before writing a soon-to-be hit song, or an architect who designs an edifice that will be marveled at for years to come, the quest and need for inspiration are directly associated with our quest for success, purpose and the pursuit of joy and happiness.

What God Has Done is a book inspired by an array of personal experiences, testimonies, and revelations that has written itself categorically over the years. I felt moved and compelled to share this body of work, as it is my fundamental notion that what we as individuals go through in this life—what we learn from, overcome, and are encouraged by—is not solely for our benefit but also for uplifting others, especially those in their times of need if we truly are our brother's keeper. The title of this book in itself is my way of suggesting, through a collection of reflective thoughts, themes, and original motivational passages and song lyrics, that although we may face challenging times, there is an uplifting spirit in and around all of us that prevails once we tap into it. Therefore, through it all, no matter what bind we may find ourselves in, if we keep the faith and do our part with the favor of God at the helm, we can claim that the victory is already won by simply realizing what God has done.

I have had very humble beginnings, for which I make no pardons or excuses but in which I take great pride. Good, bad, or indifferent, we are all the sum of our experiences, travels, areas of training and expertise, what inspires us, who inspires us, our choices, and choices made for us. A significant portion of my life, who I am today and who I strive to be, was shaped along the way by a variety of experiences, hurdles, and those who provided guidance and encouragement. Some of my experiences and lessons learned, as well as many significant others I have been impacted by along the way, have brought joy, laughter, tears, upheaval, pain, pleasure, challenges, and accomplishments.

I was born in the small southern town of Lake Village, Arkansas, in the mid-'60s. I spent the first few months of life in and around 603 Gum Street in Lake Village. Although I spent nearly every summer until entering high school down south with my grandmother, my younger brother Ricky, cousin Sheldon, and relatives in Dermott, Arkadelphia, Star City and Lake Village, Arkansas, I grew up on Churchill Avenue off of East 105th Street, near Superior, in the Glenville neighborhood of Cleveland, Ohio.

As a kid, I was small and skinny with braces, glasses and a short fro. I enjoyed listening to music, writing poetry and my piano lessons both privately from a neighbor down the street and at Rainey Institute. I loved hanging out and playing sports with longtime friends since preschool school, Roland Osborn, Dale Morgan and Wallace Riase and was moderately serious about my studies. In my neighborhood, I was outgoing and popular amongst my friends. I recall, however, receiving a fair share of teasing and bullying through my early adolescent years. I was in the first busing class during the desegregating of Cleveland Public Schools which was a most memorable but challenging time. There was a lot of anxiety, upheaval, unrest and uncertainty during my 9th grade and high school school years as east side and west side students of Cleveland would 'cross the bridge' for the first time to attend school together. I will cherish however, my years at Harry E. Davis Jr. High School and 'Dear Old' West Tech High School forever and the friendships that I've maintained since then in classmates such as Michael Watson and Mark Black. These are valued friendships I may have never known or established if not for the Cleveland desegregation experience in 1979.

I would learn during my sophomore year at Ohio University that I was adopted—and that I was the last to know in a large family and close-knit community. It was eventually revealed to me that my parents who raised me were actually my grandparents, who adopted me at age three. One of my five "sisters"—or who I grew up believing was my sister—was actually my mother. For me as a nineteen-year-old, this disclosure was quite devastating, and confusing. I look back on how that single turn of events was a pivotal and defining moment for me emotionally and realize that there are still surrounding circumstances and sentiments related to that part of my history that could literally be a book unto itself. Though *What God Has Done* is not a book about my life per se, it references many of my journeys and moments that I wish to share and offer as tools to help others pursue purpose and perseverance, and to inspire readers to seek a closer walk and personal relationship with God. It is my hope that some experiences I share throughout these pages may be just what someone needs to hear, visualize, or internalize. I hope there is something stated or shared in this book that will help you or someone else elevate to a higher sense of consciousness, awareness, self-reflection, understanding, trust in and dependency on God.

What God Has Done is my reflective montage of moments from a variety of personal experiences, original quotations, and inspirational anecdotes for daily living and application. I am not a professional counselor, philosopher, biblical scholar, or theologian, and I may not even be the sharpest tack in the drawer. However, there have been quiet and reflective moments—select stanzas, tests, testimonies, and turning points—in my life that have motivated, inspired, and uplifted me through some rather difficult times. I hope that a few of my shared experiences may also have an impact on and/or play a role in uplifting others. This, my first book, is in response to a calling I have answered at a critical turning point in my life to be more open and transparent about my life—not in a tell-all, "tell on," or epic sense but to the degree that passages I share may provide a glimpse of hope and inspiration to someone at just the right time or critical juncture in his or her life. I ultimately seek to share and tell of what God has done for me. Even the very cover that I selected for this book is representative of a transformation, a new beginning, and the realization that through the favor of God, the heavens are the limit. As I was relocating back to my native Cleveland, Ohio, after spending nearly three years in the San Francisco Bay Area, I looked out the window of the plane from my seat and snapped the image you see on the cover of this book with my cell phone in awe and amazement of the beauty, majesty, love, depth, and power of God.

I am most humbled to be able to share these select themes and expressions with you. Within *What God Has Done* rest a few chapters from my perspective that may have some positive impact on you or give you insight throughout your day and hours of meditation. As sure as we are all unique individuals with diverse experiences, backgrounds, and influences, my faith has revealed that we are purposefully created in the image of God. The ultimate inspiration and roadmap for successful living—in mind, body, and spirit—are embedded in His infallible and Holy Word. We have all been called to bear one another's burdens with a spirit of love, concern, and compassion—which is a product of divine inspiration.

When I decided to record my thoughts in this book, I went back and forth in my mind. I debated whether it should simply be a collection of sayings to inspire others versus scenarios, situations, and personal accounts that have brought me inspiration and strengthened my faith walk over the years when I needed it most. In the final analysis, after going to God in prayer, I was led to make an attempt at both. It is my sincere hope that something I faced or experienced may bring inspiration, comfort, guidance, and encouragement to others at a similar point in life or in their decision making.

I hope you will find a moving, thought-provoking, applicable or interesting passage that resonates within your spirit. If something I captured in this book helps to make a difference, brightens a day, strengthens your faith walk with God, makes you smile, brings a circumstance you are facing into clearer focus, or helps you to realize that no matter what the situation, you are not alone then mission accomplished! From my personal growth, I unveil and share words placed in my heart that at times may be difficult for me to reflect on. There are some areas in my life where I am still healing and where I am still a work in progress. I have no doubt you can identify with this as you reflect on your own journey. Our all-knowing, almighty, all-loving God is aware of our challenges and circumstances as well as the desires of our heart all while speaking at times through the obstacles, experiences, challenges, and outcomes of others.

ONE

Trust Is a Must

Trust is an invaluable asset and a precious commodity that should never be underappreciated and taken lightly or for granted. I describe trust as an asset because not everyone necessarily possesses it, develops it, or has earned it. It is not always equally valued or exchanged. Often we struggle with even identifying that which is trustworthy. Trust is also a virtue that sometimes multiplies, divides, remains constant, or depreciates, but once it exists—by being earned or given freely—it is as priceless as any precious metal, stone, or jewel. The element of trust comprises a collage of characteristics including openness, listening, and communication and possessing a firm foundation, though it may present itself on its own merit without conditions. We trust in some form or fashion daily, often without giving it much thought, hesitation, or consideration.

For instance, when crossing a bridge (I crossed the impressive six-mile Bay Bridge on many occasions while living in the San Francisco Bay Area), I had to trust that it was sturdy and would provide safe passage. When our children, grandchildren, nieces, or nephews leave for school each morning or go to the mall with friends on a sunny Saturday afternoon, we trust that they will return home safely to us without hurt, harm, or danger. We trust that the food we purchase is well prepared, tested, certified, and inspected and that it will not make us ill. We trust our doctors and lawyers, as well as other professionals from whom we seek wise counsel and expert services, to act and advocate in our best interest with excellence, precision, and in confidence. We trust our spouses and significant others with our deepest thoughts and feelings—and first and foremost to be faithful to us with unconditional love, compassion, and fidelity. We even trust the walls around us with our very lives and treasures to protect us and give us a sense of solace and security. Above all, I am learning by day and night to trust something even more than all of the aforementioned combined and then some; I am trusting in God. A God we cannot see, but, as far as the eye can see, there is indisputable evidence of His grace, presence, miracles, mercy and the outcomes of His favor. A God whose voice, though not audible, speaks to us loud and clear, even when we are at rest or too busy for devotion or to spend quality time in fellowship with Him or to meditate on Him. A God we cannot touch, yet all He touches has incomparable impact on us, both directly and indirectly, as we feel His omnipresence. Yes, trust is a mighty and powerful asset when you have it, but if you don't possess a sense of trust, and a high level of it, you have to ask yourself, "What do I really have?"

I speak from a myriad of experiences when I submit to you that I have not always understood, appreciated, valued, or honored being the recipient of someone's trust. I have regrettably and inexcusably stumbled and taken missteps in the area of trust throughout my lifetime as it relates to romantic relationships and marriage, for instance. In retrospect, there are so many things I would do differently if I knew what I know now, like how to be faithful in a marriage, how to love a wife like Christ loves the Church, and how to be appreciative, humble and honest about my feelings while respecting the feelings of others. How to realize that it is an honor to have in your possession and hold close to you the loving heart that someone has entrusted to your hands and care. How to not view the grass as being greener on the other side and to trust my instincts when I am faced with clear choices between what's right and what's wrong.

I got married and started a family at a very young age. I had a loving wife, who did all she could to keep the family together and strong. With only myself to blame, I did the opposite throughout the seven-year marriage by committing acts of infidelity and mistrust and yielding to lustful ways. I steadfastly pursued my personal goals, ambitions, and dreams. Although well intentioned, I too often neglected to be God-centered and to prioritize quality time with my young family. The breaking of the wedding vows I exchanged before God, abandoning the principles of prayer I was raised on and the selfish, immature choices I made led to the breakup of our family unit.

I trust that even though I might not have always been at my best, the best is yet to come through my evolving transformation and my trust in God. We may not be able to go back in time and rewrite the history of missteps, mistakes or missed opportunities in our choices, but a new chapter in life can be written that is built on truth, trust, humility, integrity, forgiveness, repentance, restoration, and unconditional love.

Though today has never been seen before except by God, who alone winds the hands of time, it could very well be the day that brings all you have hoped for and more than you could have ever imagined. Choose today to acknowledge or address any issues you may have with trust or being trustworthy. Just as the sun knows that moonlight will soon follow, and birds trust that there will be wind beneath their wings to fly, be encouraged. Trust, be still, and know that He is God.

Two

When All Is Said and Done

*L*et your hurdles be what challenge you to leap to even higher heights and raised expectations.

Let your obstacles be what position you to discover new pathways toward your purpose.

Let your disappointments be what propel you to a state of mind where you still do your best and settle for nothing less.

Let your frustrations be what cause you to focus with precision on the details, stepping stones, and building blocks toward your destiny.

Let your pain be what gives birth to new horizons, new beginnings, renewed strength, revived faith, and a relentless determination toward and dependency on God.

Let your passion and love for life be what motivate you to motivate and stand in the gap for others.

Let your efforts, preparation, and faith today be what prepare you for the favor God has in store for you tomorrow.

Let these words inspire you long enough to realize, tap into, and unleash your greatness and your God-given genius.

Let your armor, sword, and battle cry be the infallible word of God, which has withstood the test of time.

THREE

The Ultimate Relationship

*P*eace within, joy within, faith within, and strength within can all be measured by the ultimate relationship we are in with God. In His own appointed time, He sends us people or allows our paths to cross and intersect with those who greatly impact our lives, desires, and decisions. Without the ultimate relationship with God as the anchor, rudder, wind, and sail on the voyage of life, we cannot truly reach the virtues or preappointed destinations that He would have us reach. Yes, we look to, rely on and hold dear to our friends, spouses, and significant others, faith community, children, careers, social networks, and so many other people or things for joy, fulfillment of our needs, a sense of belonging, and sustenance. I submit to you, however (and I start with myself), that we must do more to establish that ultimate relationship with a God who fulfills all our needs, is never too busy, never sleeps, never slumbers, and will never let us down. He knows our each and every need before we even ask. So as we grow and look within to see where we are on our personal pathways in life, we are to be reminded that the ultimate relationship lies with a closer walk—and the quality time we spend in fellowship, praising, worshiping, and in meditation—with God. Even when we are faced with tragic and inexplicable turns of events, pain and loss, we must still lean on and trust in our relationship and union with God and know that His omnipotence reigns and He is still on the throne and in control. We must also be cognizant of any distractions, conflictions, or hindrances that come between us and establishing that ultimate relationship with Him. In today's world, it is easy to be overcome with ambition, personal pursuits, and the search for gratification. With a heightened focus on the things that truly matter, we come to realize that it is God's grace, protection and favor and our ultimate relationship with Him—through His love everlasting—that we could not venture without.

Four

God's Favor: The Main Ingredient for Success

*Y*ou may have life all figured out, all mapped out, and all planned out. You may have read all the bestselling self-help and how-to-be-successful books, and everything appears to be going as planned according to *your* schedule, timeline, or vision board. However, you may have left out the one main ingredient in your recipe for reaching your goals: God's favor. It is the favor of God, His perfect will, and how your steps were ordered before the earth was even formed that must first and foremost be acknowledged, recognized, and realized. It is easy to think it is "we" when it is actually "He" that makes it all happen. I do not want to look lightly upon anyone's hard work, sacrifice, accolades, credentials, drive or determination, but whether you have been given an opportunity or have created or sought an opportunity for yourself or for others, the *real* opportunity is one that receives the favor of God. How do you know that what you are doing or have accomplished is a product of God's favor? You know this by measuring your outcomes, your roadmap, and your pathways (how did you get to where you are?) and seeing if your actions, diligence, and motivations line up with the word and will of God.

I am grateful for free will and the gifts, talents, opportunities, and abilities He bestows upon us. Yes, there are those who do not acknowledge His favor, His omnipresence, or His power, yet they appear to be the beneficiaries of favorable results, rewards, elevation, increases, and outcomes. This would be consistent with the fact that it rains on the just as well as the unjust. I am conscious of and humbled to know His power from the words of the song "He," by Al Hibbler, which my grandfather sang to me when I was a child:

> *He can change the tides and calm the angry seas;*
> *He alone decides who writes the symphonies;*
> *He alone knows where to find the rainbow's end;*
> *He alone can see what lies beyond the bend;*
> *He can touch a tree and turn the leaves to gold;*
> *He knows every lie both you and I have told;*
> *Though it makes Him sad to see the way we live,*
> *He'll always say, "I forgive."*

When I was young, I did not fully understand the meaning of those words my grandfather would sing in his soothing first tenor voice, but what this verse says to me today is that when God lends His favor, it is greater than and will out-weigh, outlast, outperform and outproduce any plan, pursuit, or creation I could ever imagine or dream of for my life. So in all you do and in all your preparation, planning, and petition-ing, do not neglect to seek and ask for God's favor, the main ingredient for success.

FIVE

Just Because

*N*ow some of you may be hopeless romantics or never miss the chance to bring a smile to someone's face by remembering their birthdays, Valentine's Day, (Sweetest Day for you Ohioans like me), Mother's Day, anniversaries, accomplishments or any of the many red letter days throughout the year. Days and special occasions on which we express our appreciation with the ever-faithful, never-failing flower may only come a few times a year. However, what if we established a sincere heart-felt practice of giving that special someone flowers *just because*, not just because it's the day when you're supposed to give flowers!

The endearing act of giving flowers is not just limited to giving the physical flower or having them delivered; there are symbolic flowers, too, and expressions that emote and resonate the same feelings, if not stronger. These flowers speak to the heart with a chorus that says, "I recognize; I appreciate; I dedicate; I care; I love; I thank you, I celebrate you; I celebrate us...*just because*." Even a morning greeting to or a goodnight embrace of that loved one, parent, or child who you know is the air you breathe and without whom you could not live or be without, that's giving a flower. Believe it or not, that encouraging word to someone who feels as if there is no tomorrow elevates and uplifts his or her spirit and gives him or her a reason for being, a reason to carry on and not give up—you've given that person a flower. That smile to a child, youth or young adult that reinforces how proud you are of him or her and his or her efforts, and for at least trying and putting forth his or her best, that, too, is giving a flower.

I am certain there are those who have crossed our paths throughout our lives, and we would give anything to hand them just one more flower if we could. Therefore, it is crucial and critical not to forgo opportunities and moments to give flowers of kindness, congeniality, affinity, and affection through our actions, words, expressions, and sentiments... *just because*. More often, we need to make and take the time out of our busy lives and schedules to not just stop and smell the roses but to pause if just for a moment to be a rose to someone else—mainly because we never know what tomorrow holds or may bring. If I had known twenty-two years ago, when I was playing basketball on that sunny, summer Wednesday afternoon with my younger brother Clint at age nineteen, that it would be the last time we would laugh and play together as a result of his untimely death three days later, I would have given him flowers that day *just because*. If I had known that the last time I saw my grandmother would be the final time I'd ever see her until her homegoing celebration, I would have given her flowers that day *just because*.

If you take a real, honest, and reflective look back on your life, I am certain there is someone you wish you had given flowers to more often than you did, if you did at all, *just because*. Now the message behind this passage is not meant to be a sad one but one of awakening. It is simply meant to encourage you to be mindful that today, which God has blessed you to see, provides you with a new opportunity to not wait for a holiday to celebrate what someone means to you. Please, from this day on, do not take another precious moment above ground for granted despite how busy, obligated, driven, consumed, stressed, or in survival mode you may be. Let's face it: in the final analysis of it all, each of us is simply a vapor, a passing mist in the eyes of God among an infinite universe that spans endlessly in every direction. Yet He knows what is on our plates and how much we can bear, just as He knows what we are faced with and are up against. He also lets us know that He loves us...*just because*.

After you have read this chapter, reach out to someone with love and give that person flowers today...*just because*. If you are not in a position to purchase or deliver a flower, email, text, draw a picture of a flower with a crayon or marker or forward the image of a flower as a dear friend did for me after first reading this chapter. When the recipient asks you, "What are these flowers for?" or "What did I do to deserve them?"—even if he or she asks, "What did *you* do?"—simply reply with a smile, "These flowers are just because I think you are special" or "Just because I love you."

Six

The Answer May Be at Your Fingertips

What an amazing era in which to be alive, with so much access and information at the click of a mouse, the touch of a screen, and the scroll of a cursor. Words and references now exist that just a couple of generations ago, even a few years ago were not in the dictionary, in our vocabularies, nor readily used and regarded as they are today. Via computers, tablets, and/or mobile devices, there is not much you can't find out, research, cross check, or ascertain within seconds through technology, downloadable applications, and the World Wide Web. Of course, the information has to be imported at some point in order to be retrieved, but, today, that is a minor technicality.

When I was a little boy, I remember being in the house with my grandmother on one particular day when she was frantically looking for her glasses. I recall walking into the room to offer to help her find them, when I noticed that they were resting atop her hair. We laughed about it, and she said with a smile, "Just wait…one day you are going to be old like Mama, and your glasses are going to be right there in front of you too." Now, a few months shy of turning fifty is not old, but something similar happened to me just the other day. My search, however, was for the cable TV remote—only I realized that the one I was looking for was right there in front of me the whole time.

This was also my life-changing experience in 1989. I was looking so hard and so diligently for answers about my paternal family history—only to find out that the answers were right there at my fingertips. Since my sophomore year in college, when I learned I was adopted, I prayed to God for a breakthrough, leads, a picture, or anything that would give me some satisfaction about or insight into the paternal side of my family tree. Not many could or were willing to help fill that void or begin to connect the dots for me, including my grandparents or my mother. This was extremely frustrating but not to the point where I could not function, though it would begin to affect me emotionally in ways that are hard to describe. Let me be clear however…my desire to research and find information that would lead me to my paternal side did not diminish the love I had for the family that reared me, the loving maternal side of my family I was born into and the only family I knew. But Stevie Wonder, who I saw perform live at the former Front Row Theatre a few years prior in Greater Cleveland, had a song out at the time that summarized my feelings in one word…"Whereabouts". As the song posed the question, 'where is the missing one?'…this would be one of the questions about my life amongst many, that I was determined to find the answer to regardless the cost, risk factors, response or unknown outcome.

Only God knew my gazes up at the ceiling in the middle of the night and the inquisitive thoughts that would follow. I would try to picture for years what my biological father looked like by looking intensely at myself in the mirror. I wondered about his mannerism, style of dress, personality, demeanor and what he might have been like before he passed away in 1975. He was a U.S. Navy Seaman and also served his country honorably in Vietnam in the U.S. Army. In my quiet moments, I would wonder if he had a family or other children like me. I am sure God gives us our hearts' desires, because just as both my curiosity and frustration began to rival and reach a peak when I was twenty-four years old, I had a breakthrough that ended up being right at my fingertips. I refused to believe there was no trace of my father, his memory or the paternal side of my family. I knew the name of my biological father's widow and began looking through the white pages for her one afternoon. *(There were no smart phones or Google for a name search in 1989 so the white pages of the telephone book was all I had to work with).*

I found his last name, 'Ward', and looked through the listings with a G, the first initial of his wife's name. I searched and then dialed them one by one. I called about five or six 'G. Wards' but to no avail. I felt saddened, dejected, disappointed, as if to arrive at a dead-end once again. I realize that life is not always fair, but it seemed unfair to me that something as simple as wanting to know who I was and to whom I was connected still seemed to be too much to ask for or have answered. This doesn't suggest that I had no sense of self, but I did not feel complete since I did not know the other half of the whole story. I had to know for myself that my life and my existence were more than just an adoption ruling, a journal entry, and the signing away of a teenage mother's legal rights so that I was raised as her little brother and the issue was never to be spoken of again. I'm just sharing with you an abbreviated backdrop of how I was made to feel for a long time. Thank God that He knows all the answers! Praise God that He hears and answers prayers, sees our pain, and knows the desires of our hearts. I dialed the very next number and asked to speak to Geneva Ward. This call would change my life instantaneously and forever more. She said she was Geneva Ward, and after nervously introducing myself, I asked if she was once married to Paul Ward. She simply replied, "Yes. Who is this?" The moment I had waited years to experience had finally come. With all my emotion, excitement, anticipation, and built-up anxiety, all I could do was hang up the phone in disbelief.

I called back immediately and apologized. She was most gracious and understanding—motherly, even. I then proceeded to relay my story as I knew it, the connection, (or should I say 'our connection'), and ultimately my quest to be connected to a part of me of which I had no knowledge. After she confirmed that she indeed had been married to Paul Ward, even at the time of his sudden death, we talked in much detail about the era in which I was born, along with sharing the few names of paternal family members and family history that I researched or had knowledge of in which she confirmed. Because I do not believe in coincidences or luck, I knew this was God's perfect timing and favor. It was a pleasant conversation that I will never forget and will always cherish, especially since I had no way of knowing how I would be received, believed or accepted. In addition to the fact that for years prior, many discussions I would initiate about my 'whereabouts' drew awkward silence, avoidance or evasive and uncomfortable volleys of questions and answers which normally left me even more confused and frustrated, yet more determined. This part of my life has many chapters involving many people I love and care for, which makes it that much more sensitive, delicate, and even emotional to talk about and reflect upon at times. Some chapters are still evolving; others are unfinished and unresolved. I've also grown to accept the reality that some chapters may never be resolved and may be closed forever. Many chapters have subsequently impacted my children over the years in more ways than one to no fault of their own.

But no chapter in this instance is greater than the desire to feel accepted, acknowledged, included and unconditionally recognized and embraced for who you are regardless of how you came to be. I am not ashamed to admit that I felt this of myself on many occasions. I know now that for years I went through life internalizing my own 'if/then' theory. It went something like this: 'If' I was not being accepted, acknowledged or recognized for who I really was…'then' I must have been a secret and was not meant to be, or my true identity was never to be disclosed, discussed or found out, thus I was a mistake. Although the premise may have some truth, the assumption could not be more false. Someone, somewhere needs to know regarding *their* situation as I have grown to realize about mine…God makes no mistakes. God also knows, relieves and comforts our burdens when we are weary and heavy laden. Although we may feel that we don't fit, God can align and realign us according to His perfect plan, perfect will and divine purpose.

However, what I will say to those who are frustrated and feel they are at the end of their ropes and have done all they know how to do is what a mighty God we serve! To someone who feels there is a missing chapter in his or her life, be patient and don't give up; God can connect the dots for you in His appointed time and season. For someone reading this chapter or for someone whom you may want to share my experience with who feels they are misunderstood, unaccepted or they feel alone, rejected or isolated as if the world is evolving without them and no one seems to relate to their pain, struggle or reality…know that God does and is the ultimate comforter. There comes a time when simply 'accepting your circumstance and moving on' is a layered, day-to-day process that is easier said than done. I've had 'just move on' said to me more times than not since learning I was adopted my sophomore year in college. Persevere, press on and move on yes, but sometimes you can't 'move on' until you 'move over' and let God take the lead, guide and control which delivers you to the answers you've been seeking with a sense of solace and compassion that only He can provide. After years of unanswered questions. After years of so many things I thought to be true but were not the case. After years and tears of dead-end leads, discouragement even ridicule, at my fingertips I was led to the unsuspecting, yet accepting wife and family of a man I never knew, but who was my biological father. As I credit the favor of God and that I refused to give up, the outcome was I met three younger brothers—Paul, Van, and William—I never knew I had but to whom I am as close to as if we had grown up together all of our lives; and I was accepted into an extended family that embraced me, claimed me, and included me unconditionally from day one. I recognize that this outcome could have gone totally different and another way. This is why I am humbled to know that our amazing God placed all of this and a most favorable outcome at my very fingertips.

Also placed at my fingertips would be my paternal cousin 'Sunny' who is now deceased, but was introduced to me when I was about 20 years old by my maternal 'brother/uncle' Wallis. The two of them went to high school together and Wallis new all along that Sunny and I were related through my biological father, who once lived just three blocks away from our house on the corner of East 105 street and Wade Park. Wallis also knew of my love for music, playing the piano and my aspirations of one day becoming a great songwriter and producer. Wallis was obviously aware that my cousin Sunny was affiliated with a popular local record company and recording studio at the time in Cleveland, Time Traxx Records. Out of the blue, as I can remember as if it were yesterday, Wallis said to me he was 'taking me to meet my cousin today'. To place this is context, it was no secret then I was in high pursuit of any information that would satisfy questions I had about my paternal family history and more importantly any lead that would produce a simple picture of my biological father and my 'whereabouts'. My introduction to Sunny revealed to me significant paternal family history I had long wondered and inquired about, including the discovery that I had other siblings and an uncle that lived nearby in a Cleveland east side neighborhood. I would also learn of and meet paternal cousins living in the Cleveland Area and an aunt residing in Cincinnati, Ohio.

Needless to say, what began as another long-awaited discovery for me during that anxious time, ended on a sad and devastating note. Sunny eventually arranged for me to meet my father's older brother Clarence in which I was able to talk with him at great length about my father and other family history on my paternal side. The process of Clarence and me getting to know each other however was short lived as he would face a tragic and untimely death. He was shot and killed not far from his apartment in Cleveland one morning a few years after I met him. I have no doubt that before his murder, he held the key to a lot of unanswered questions I would still have. During one of our conversations, Clarence shared with me that my father once made reference to me, which further confirmed for me that my father knew *of* me and that I existed. I can't describe how important that alone is for me to know. Uncle Clarence represented more than just an Uncle I never knew and he is greatly missed.

Nonetheless, God also placed me into the loving and caring hands of the maternal side of my family, from whom I received a strong, structured, and loving foundation. I dearly love the family that raised me and embodies all my memories from childhood through my adolescence, spent with my younger brother Ric, little sister Kim ("B"), and her twin, the late Clinton Hall Jr. along with a host of relatives spanning from Cleveland to Arkansas and beyond. I am truly blessed to have and treasure all that makes up our large family.

To those who may be able to relate to this event or are walking in similar shoes right this second, shedding the same tears and wanting to be accepted for who they are, God is not only the answer, but the answer to what you desire may not be as far out of reach as you may think. It may be right at your fingertips. Just ask, trust, and believe that God will guide your heart and your hand.

SEVEN

You Have Found the Feather...
Now Bring Back the Bird

I have always been a fan of metaphors. Even as a student at West Tech High School in Cleveland, where I wrote my sports column, "The Ivory Tower," for the school newspaper, I can remember writing with colorful words and symbolic phrases. Also, as a songwriter, I know that nothing graces a memorable melody more passionately than metaphors that allow the listener to visually drift into the author's vision of artistic and creative lyrical comparisons. Now that you've sat patiently through my English lesson, I say congratulations to you!

You've worked hard, you've made great strides and progress, and you've accomplished something significant of which to be proud. It may be that promotion or merit raise you recently received at your job. Maybe you've studied long and hard and earned an "A" on your final, passed the Bar Exam or have graduated proudly with that much-anticipated degree or certification in hand. Through much sacrifice, investment, and planning, someone has successfully opened a new business or entered into a promising joint venture. Maybe you've just been appointed to a prestigious board of directors, where you now can help move an organization forward and lend your expertise to its mission. With that said, here's the metaphor: you have found the feather; now I challenge you to bring back the bird.

So, then, what is the feather, and what is the bird in this passage? First, let me state that by using the symbol of the feather, I am not suggesting that your accomplishment represents anything lightweight, insignificant, or without merit. What I am suggesting is the total opposite. The feather on a bird—especially those like eagles that are synonymous with soaring, having laser-precision vision and focus, and reaching enormous heights—is a wondrous thing and something to be admired, as is the case with your accomplishment.

So when I say, "You have found the feather; now bring back the bird," the feather you have found represents your hard work, your preparation, and ultimately your liftoff, which is what encourages, inspires, motivates, and elevates you to the next level. The feather also represents your determination, commitment, and resolve to overcome obstacles as you make incremental progress and reach higher heights. With that said, if all of this is represented by the feather then imagine what the bird symbolizes.

In this metaphor, the bird represents your goals, positive outcomes, dreams, and finally your reward, which is your success. What I would like to emphasize to encourage you on your journey and pursuit of purpose is *how* you go about bringing back the bird.

First, you must have self-confidence to recognize your full potential and have faith in your God-given abilities and what He can do as the head of your life. Far too many people, especially young ones, don't believe in themselves, nor do they have a strong sense of who they are or *whose they are*. We may identify ourselves as many things to many people, but first and foremost we should identify ourselves as children of God, therefore making us heirs to His goodness, transforming grace, and favor in helping with the hearts' desires. In such a competitive world, where life is constantly moving at the speed of business, many of us lack the self-confidence, self-esteem, motivation, and belief that if you prepare yourself, coupled with the favor of God, you can do anything to which you set your mind. So the first step in bringing back the bird is to believe in yourself and in what it means to be a child of God.

Second, you must realize, awaken, activate, and release your greatness and the genius within. God made each of us in a unique way and in His own image. No two of us are the same, and He alone knows the number of hairs on our heads. (I just had to interject again how awesome our God is.) We all have individual talents, gifts, and contributions that we are predestined to fulfill and bring to fruition. Furthermore, within us lies a degree of greatness and genius if only we have the foundation, foresight, and fortitude to tap into it. The definition of "genius" is simple: an exceptional intellectual capacity, especially as shown in creative and original work. This may speak directly to you since you possess traits of greatness and genius. But the questions remain: Do you realize it? Have you reeled it in, awakened, and released your God-given ability? Have you successfully activated the ingenuity and excellence that He had bestowed upon you before the earth was even formed?

Some may say they are not the best academically or have not performed well in school or in their chosen professions. I say, however, that there is still greatness in you. Awaken the genius within! If you have worked tirelessly for that promotion or title while seeing others advance around you, I say your season is coming, but God says, "You shall reap a harvest of blessings if you faint not." (Galatians 6:9). To those who feel that their business ventures are not where they want them to be or if you have not been as successful as an entrepreneur as you had envisioned, I say to you don't give up. In your determination, preparedness, and vision, there is still greatness in you. Awaken the genius within! Although you may still be a work in progress in many aspects of your life, as I am, I maintain that there is greatness inside of you as our Father in heaven is the author of the universe. What could be greater than that? Your greatness and your genius must be realized, reeled in, awakened, activated, and released.

Finally, as you have found the feather and seek to bring back the bird, you must develop your idea, plan, or vision, conduct the necessary research and due diligence, seek proper guidance and wise counsel, and then execute—but always with a purpose. I'm sure you've heard this statement before: we don't plan to fail; we fail to plan. Although it may take time, preparation, and long hours of trial and error, developing your plan of action is a vital step in any successful endeavor or pursuit. I would just encourage you to include God in the plan as you seek His voice, guidance, countenance, favor, and purpose for your life.

Professionally, I work tirelessly to provide programing and exposure opportunities to help close the achievement gap and increase high school graduation rates amongst targeted youth in Cuyahoga County, Ohio, and beyond. The planning, data collection, research, preparation, and presentation necessary prior to launching the initiative was very involved but all worth it in the end. It did not begin to all come together, however, until I began to realize that my quests were beginning to align with what I believe to be one of God's purposes for my life.

I am very careful not to minimize or shortcut all that is required in reaching your goals, positive outcomes, dreams, and reward, which is your success. I simply want to encourage you and illustrate through this metaphor that you should continue on your pathway to excellence even after accomplishing your initial triumph. You are just beginning to scratch the surface of what God wants to bless you with and has in store for you. His blessings and favor on your life's endeavors may have a broader purpose than you realize. Yes, we will have ambitions, have to provide and make a living, and even have lists of personal goals, well-thought-out strategic plans, and vision boards. God, however, may very well be blessing or positioning you in order for you to be a blessing and encouragement to someone else on whom He has His hands. So as your steps are ordered, remember to have self-confidence and recognize your full potential and God-given abilities. Realize, reel in, awaken, activate, and release your greatness and your genius within; develop your ideas and execute your plan or vision with God's purpose for your life in mind.

Once again, congratulations on your accomplishments. You have found the feather. Now I challenge you to bring back the bird.

EIGHT

Oh, to Dance with My Grandparents Again

I remember growing up, being raised by my grandparents, and being the only child still at home. I didn't learn I was adopted until I was nineteen, and, to this day, that is an ever-evolving story with many, many chapters. Nonetheless, I recall being a child preparing for church on Sunday morning. I did not know at the time what my grandparents were really preparing me for and instilling in me. We would sometimes catch two CTS or RTA buses to Antioch Baptist Church on East 89th and Cedar Avenue in Cleveland. (That's when a neighbor or a church member did not give us a ride to church as my grandparents did not drive). On many Sunday mornings, my grandfather and I would walk for about thirty minutes to Sunday school. This seemed like a hundred miles to an eight- or nine-year-old boy who wanted to stay in bed and watch cartoons. My grandfather was about six-foot-two, so I probably took two or three steps for each of his.

I would often rather stay home and watch television (one of the three channels the TV would get with a pair of pliers as the remote) or play outside with some of my friends who did not have to go to church on Sunday mornings for some reason. I wondered how they could be so lucky. But I can hear my grandfather say to me, "Robert, you don't miss school or playing ball outside after school. I don't miss work, nor am I late to work, so we are not going to miss church." That was usually the last word on the matter, especially if he started the sentence with "Robert"; everyone else in the family called me by my nickname, Bobby. I wonder if any of this sounds remotely familiar to you.

Now fast forward to our routines today. It's so amazing how we are consciously on time for our business meetings, to catch a flight, to be in front of the television when our favorite show or sporting event comes on, or we even arrive to concerts, plays, conferences, and comedy shows an hour early for the best seats in the house, yet we often go to the House of the Lord—He who makes a way for it all—to worship when we feel like it, *if* we feel like it…yours truly included. I, too, am a work in progress as I am sometimes guilty of placing worshiping God in the "other" category as if He were on a to-do list or my weekly agenda instead of referring to my childhood example modeled by my grandparents, who made spending quality time with God a priority with a prominent place in our lives. I thank God for the loving memories of my grandparents and for them taking me to Sunday school and church when I didn't understand the importance of going. They would also teach me by example that worshiping, praising and serving God and His people does not end with the benediction after Sunday service, but is to be continued throughout the week. Though they both have gone home to be with the Lord, I was able to thank them before they passed away for adopting me after raising six children of their own and doing the best they knew how in raising me and providing me with a home filled with love and structure. Training me in the way I should go was their guidance and teaching, and most of all they laid a solid foundation for me that I reflect upon to this very day. Things were not perfect by far. My grandparents were not perfect, as none of us is. There were hard times, even confusing times, but it was a humbling and memorable part of my life when I was still able to be a child and enjoy much of my childhood. My grandfather had high academic standards for me and was quite the disciplinarian and a stickler for order, respect, and structure. He was very hard on me, but understanding the era in which he was raised during the Great Depression and in the turbulent Jim Crow south, I have grown to appreciate his intentions of wanting the best for me.

I love and miss them for this and for so much more. Oh, to dance with my grandparents again! If you are blessed and fortunate enough to still have your parents, grandparents, foster parents, adoptive parents, aunts, uncles, mentors or those significant adults who raised you, contributed to your success, or stood in the gap and did their best to make you your best, please dance with them today for me.

Nine

"May I Have Your Attention, Please?" —God

*H*ave you ever felt as if God was saying to you, "Okay, now that I have your undivided attention…"? Well, that was exactly how I felt one day while attending The Ohio State University and UC Berkeley football game in Berkeley, California, one Saturday when I was living in the San Francisco Bay Area. My right eye became so irritated and swollen during the game that I could barely focus on the field, let alone the game. It was so painful that even my sunglasses did not prevent the increased sensitivity to light I was experiencing. At first I thought I might have had my contacts in for too long or didn't disinfect them thoroughly. Or after losing then regaining sight in my left eye the year before as a result of a detached retina, I thought my right eye might have been showing similar signs of what I had previously experienced.

(Of course, that was "Dr. Bob" trying to rationalize sitting through The Ohio State football game despite his growing pain and eye discomfort!)

By the time my girlfriend and I got to the apartment, my eye was in so much pain and so irritated. I seriously contemplated going to the emergency room, but when my "macho man—I can take the pain" mindset kicked in, all I could do was put a cold compress on my eye after taking my contacts out. I then proceeded to lie down and pray for relief. (To any young person reading this book, don't hesitate to tell your parents or other adults or seek medical care if you have any pain or discomfort associated with your eyes or your vision.) Needless to say, at that very instant I could literally hear a voice say to me, "Okay, now that I have your undivided attention…"

As I sought relief and tried to doze off to sleep, I took that voice to be the spirit of God saying to me unequivocally, "There will be no Facebook, Instagram, surfing the Internet, or text messaging this evening. There will be no movie watching or ESPN either. There will be no checking email or phone messages you missed while at the football game. (Yes, the Buckeyes won by the way…O-H!) You will spend this time with Me in silence, in reflection, in meditation, in devotion, period."

How often do we complete all the tasks we have every day: work, our normal routines, business activities, leisure activities, fitness regimens? We're nonstop, but as soon as we are stricken with illness or fatigue, or we are in over our heads, we find time to cry out, "Lord, help me!" Our God is an awesome God, but according to my faith and belief, He is also a jealous God. What He said to me through my ordeal that day was, "Bobby, spend less time doing everything else under the sun that you want to do and more quality time with Me, your God. Spend some time in My *Word* aside from the times you want or need something." This voice resonated within me. Yes, there are times when God requires our undivided attention, when His voice and fellowship with us alone prevail and take precedence.

Rest assured, I will pay closer attention to my eyes and have my vision checked periodically as prescribed. I will also pay closer attention to and improve upon my personal relationship with God and put into perspective all the things I am guilty of putting before the One who gives and restores sight. God should not be someone that we fit into our busy schedules, place on our check-off lists, or click on an iPhone app as we surf to see what's out there or who's online to send an instant message to or chat with.

The air, water, sunlight, sustenance, and saving grace He provides should be sufficient enough to make Him a necessary part of our daily lives. I wonder what it will take for God to gain your undivided attention today.

You have to ask yourself if the setbacks that you may be experiencing or going through could be occurring for more reasons than you realize. Just like in my favorite scene and song from the classic movie *The Color Purple*, what if "God is trying to tell you something"?

TEN

In Your Mirror

What do you see when you look in the mirror every day? Obviously, there are many observations one can make, whether consciously or subconsciously, visually or beneath the surface. Some observations are based on physical traits, and some are emotional and/or psychological. Other observations may be reflective or retrospective and are often based on our current situations and circumstances. We see changes we want to make in our appearance or progress we've made toward personal physical goals. We may see worry around our eyes as a result of stressful situations or a zest for life on our faces as everything may be bright, sunny, and overflowing with an abundance of joy and happiness. Sometimes in our mirror images we will find the wear and tear from what we've been through or the joy from within that we experience from life's treasures. In your mirror, you may gaze upon remnants of your youth as well as glance into your ever-evolving maturity and the inevitable aging process. If you look closely enough in your mirror, you might even capture in your eyes that glow or gleam that you or others see as a direct or indirect result of that special someone in your life—you know that warm and fuzzy look that you can't hide when your happiness is written all over your face. However, in your mirror—whether it is round, rectangular, handheld, hanging on the wall, rear view or full length—should symbolize the miraculous reality of all that God has done since the lighting of the sun. He took the time to put all of Himself into making one of you.

That alone says to me and hopefully speaks to you about how special you are in the eyes of God. Despite the changes you think you should make, the flaws you say you have, the look you aspire to attain, and even how you may feel inside, you are precious in His sight. You are made in His glorious image. He has each hair on your head numbered; therefore, you are a unique and special kind. It's troubling when I stop to think of the many people, especially young girls, who struggle with having low self-esteem and low self-worth, not realizing how beautiful they really are. It is also disheartening how the color of one's skin throughout history has been used to divide, discriminate against, persecute, enslave, profile, and deny equal opportunities to people. For those fixated on the color of one's skin as too many are in our society today, *(not anyone reading this book I am sure),* I invite you to pause and fixate on Revelations1:15 where the Lord is described as such:

'…His feet were like bronze refined in a furnace'. If you are a visual learner like myself, try placing a bronze medal in fire and let it burn for a while. Take it out and let it cool off then fixate on what color it becomes. Read again Rev. 1:15 for yourself. Then ask yourself the next time you or someone else is fixated on the color of someone's skin in a negative way, have you ever seen someone's feet a different color than their face? I'm just saying…look behind the words and find the meaning.

If only we would all recognize and internalize the fact that within all of our mirrors, there is an image of God Himself with distinct traits and characteristics that make us unique and royal. Underneath that image and below the layers of our skin is a spirit aligned with Him that gives us exclusive access to Him and all His glory. What a joy to know that as God created the heavens and the earth all in less than a week, He still took the loving time to create and breathe life into us to the extent that there are no two of us alike. He created only one of each of us equally with a preordained assignment and ordered steps that only we can walk in and fulfill.

Yes, in my mirror I see many images. I see a tall man who I resemble in my late biological father, who I have no memory of ever meeting. One of my 'sisters' shared with me the story that while we were walking near our house on Churchill Avenue one day, my late father caught up with us, confirmed who I was, and asked if he could pick me up. I was told that he kneeled down, picked me up, and asked me my name. He would talk to me for a few seconds then placed a 50 cent piece in my hand, set me down and walked away as I waved goodbye. I was told that I went into the house and said to my grandmother, 'look what that man gave me'…showing her my new coin. I'm sure for a three-year-old in 1968, there was probably not as much precaution and hesitancy about talking to a stranger as there would be today. The mind is so amazing. Although I have no recollection of him or that moment, not only have I probably subconsciously convinced myself over the years that I remember that encounter, I still catch myself looking in my mirror sometimes and reflecting on our physical resemblance. It is rather striking, which I notice from a few pictures that I have seen, as well as the mannerisms I've been told he and I share from his wife who knew him best.

I see in my mirror my birth mother, close yet so far from a true mother-son relationship for which I've always yearned and envied. As far as my memory allows me to go, I can honestly say I knew there was something different, special and unique about our relationship and interaction as a young child, but just couldn't put my finger on why this was so. When I was about eight years old, I was so mad at my grandfather one day for his firmness and heavy hand (and that is an understatement), I was fed up and planned to run away from home that night. My brilliant plan included packing my little blue suitcase which I did, place it under my bed before I went to Doan Elementary School that day, thus when my grandparents went to sleep that night, I would call my one 'sister' who for some reason appeared to be my favorite. She always seemed to pay close attention to me whenever she would visit or I would visit her. My plan was simple…she would come get me in the middle of the night and take me away to live with her. She would not have to ring the front doorbell. Did I add that my brilliant plan included me jumping down off the roof of my second floor bedroom window where her 'get-away car' would be waiting on Hull Avenue, the street behind Churchill?! (Never mind the metal fence and huge mulberry tree directly outside my window below, my plan didn't factor in those obstructions I guess. Nor did I think about until now, to simply tip-toe down the steps and quietly go out the back door). My fool-proof runaway plan was foiled however, when my grandmother found my suitcase that was in plain sight underneath my bed before I came home from school that day. She asked me why I had all my clothes and a few toys bundled up in a suitcase under my bed? I eventually told her that I was tired of getting whippings, I wanted to run away and I didn't want to live there anymore. She was ironing and without breaking her stride smiled and told me I could go if I wanted to, but couldn't take the clothes or my toys. I went upstairs to my room at a loss for words and unpacked. I guess you can say without me knowing why, even then as an 8-year-old, I saw in my mirror 'my favorite sister'. A 'sister' who I could count on to rescue me only to one day learn she was actually my mother who heard my heartbeat right along-side hers before I was born.

I continue to pray for God's favor, divine intervention, and healing in our relationship as I love my mother so and nothing will ever change that. Although I am grateful to have been adopted by my grandparents considering the complexities of the time and reared by them as their son, no legal document replaces or could ever change or substitute the desire to be loved and acknowledged by the mother who brought you into this world.

I see in my mirror my beautiful children, who I love to no end. I see precious memories as well as difficult times and many mistakes made as a father and as a young man trying to find himself over the years. I constantly strive to be better and do better as I pray that God continues to bless our relationships, close any gaps that may exist, strengthen us, and wrap us in His love and care as we all grow older. I've worked with hundreds of youth over the course of my career from serving as a group home Child Care Worker and Youth Leader, to Juvenile Detention and Correctional Officer to project managing and now directing a high school closing the achievement gap initiative. However, to each of my 5 children that I can't help but see in my mirror, I say unequivocally, I love you so, and would lay down my life for each of you and would do so many things differently if I knew the things that I know now.

I see in my mirror the sum of my choices and the choices of others that have shaped and impacted my life and reflect in part who I am today and the man I am striving to be. I see my wants and desires, passions and purpose, joys and pains, peaks and valleys, loves and losses—but through the imperfections, challenges, and triumphs, I see in my mirror the same image of God, who created the universe and took the time to create even me.

So when you look in your mirror today, look closely and realize just how special you truly are, despite it all, to be loved and touched by God Himself. See within your reflection your many redeeming qualities, attributes and the wondrous work He wants to perform in your life.

ELEVEN

We're Still Family

The breakdown of many families today can at times be associated with and attributed to some sort of disconnect in communication. Have you or a family member ever allowed an unresolved issue, an exchange of harsh words, a dispute, an argument, a misunderstanding, or a wrongdoing place weeks, months, years, or even generations of silence, conflict or avoidance between you? God ordained and placed His blessings upon the family, and it has been the enemy's full-time job to rob, kill, destroy, and tear it down ever since. Let this be the day that you break that stronghold or generations of distance, regrets, blame and upheaval. Take the first step and rise above your family differences or disputes with family members and dial their numbers or make an attempt to go visit them if possible. Send them a sincere greeting card, invite them over to talk over a meal, email them, text, in-box, video message, write a letter or poem, or send a picture—whichever is your style—to tell them you love them and want to repair the broken relationship right now rather than later.

Let that family member know you would like to begin a journey down the pathway to becoming a family again or where you can at least begin to heal and build a new set of memories based on love, trust, mutual respect, and forgiveness. Of course, this may be easier said than done, depending on the situation and depth of the family dynamic, divide, or distance.

I am very sensitive to the reality that some family situations may be so severely damaged or strained that it may require a more intense, even professional or divine, intervention. (I say this with the utmost respect and acknowledgment, careful not to minimize anyone's pain, hurt, trauma, or special circumstances that persist within family situations, especially when at the core of the dynamics is the devastation caused by abuse, neglect, and/or abandonment.)

Without question, life is too short, and tomorrow is not promised to anyone. With that said, someone reading and processing this message is broken and hurting because of a family tie or bond that has been severed, distanced, damaged, or negatively impacted. This will certainly have an impact on present relationships, choices, outlooks on life, quality of life, and future generations. What better day than today and what better time than now to reach out in love, if at all possible, with a sincere effort to take the first step in putting that relationship back together again (where appropriate)? Start with cleansing your own heart of any negative thoughts or energy and petition God to guide, comfort, and be in the midst. Give Him any load or memory that you find too heavy, hurtful, or harsh to carry on your own as He holds the weight of the whole world in the palm of His hands.

I had an older "brother," Wallis Jr., and when I was a child, I looked up to him. Due to the circumstances surrounding my adoption, he was actually my uncle. He was very much the family member with whom I spent a lot of time throughout my adolescence. We were separated in age by twenty years, and he was my idol, as older siblings often are. I also had four brothers-in-law who I looked up to, admired, and loved dearly. I can honestly say I was blessed to have positive, strong and caring male role models all around me as a child, which I know helped to shape and mold me which is critically important for a young boy to have. When it came to my brother Wallis, however, I wanted to dress like him, tilt my hat to the side like his, work out and have muscles like his, drive a car like his, and be "cool" like him. I was most impressed by him in the '70s, so you can only imagine what the clothes, cars, hat, and "cool" looked like! Nothing mattered to me then except that he was my "big brother." Despite what anyone said and despite any reputation he might have had, all I knew was how close we were. Eventually our closeness and relationship deteriorated in our adult years. It not only deteriorated, but our last few encounters were quite volatile and mean-spirited. They were filled with anger and hard words as the result of very serious unresolved family issues. He suddenly passed away not long ago, before we could reconcile after years of distance, animosity, and seriously painful issues. It's amazing how someone you looked up to and with whom you were close—someone who's every word you leaned on as a child and once held in such high esteem—can evolve into the one who disappoints and hurts you more than words can express. He and I never got the opportunity to mend the fences, right the wrongs, or try to fix what was broken in our strained relationship. Do not let my story, with which I will live forever, be yours. As long as you can breathe air and have a sound mind to formulate your thoughts and serve an interceding God, you can make that change today. Won't you at least give it a try? Although there is no guarantee that your efforts or olive branch will be received or acknowledged by the other person, at least you can rest assured that you tried, and your intentions were pure. If you do your part, and if it's God will, He will do the rest, even if it means He must soften the hardened heart of the other person long enough to receive your outstretched hands and sincerity. If the reconciliation and healing between you and that family member are truly the desires of your heart, I honestly believe God will honor your request. He will hear your prayers and bridge that gap between you and your loved one or family through His grace and His love.

I would reconcile with my brother Wallis if I could, but since I can't, I encourage someone to take that first step toward healing that family wound today. For all we know, tomorrow may never come. If you have difficulty finding the right words to say… please allow me to lend you these to start:

You might be this,
I might be that,
We might be mad,
But we're still family, and that still means the world to me.

TWELVE

Facing and Replacing Your Fears with Faith as We Seek the Face of God

*P*ublic speaking, heights, swimming, crossing large bodies of water, flying, the dark, success, escalators, needles, bees, small enclosed places, death, and crowds. What initially comes to mind when you reflect on these words? This is just a short list of a long litany of common fears and phobias that people everywhere face every day. There are even a few phobias I have never heard of or encountered before, such as globophobia, which is the fear of balloons, and anatidaephobia, which is a fear of ducks. If you are like so many others who have experienced a fear or phobia of some kind at some time in your life or even know someone who does, you would agree that it is nothing to take lightly and may even be very serious and frightening.

I am by no means qualified to psychoanalyze or break down the complexities, abnormalities, or emotional or physiological elements, effects, or constructs relating to fear. However, as humans, none of us is exempt or immune from having some sort of fear. There may be an area or instance in which we are overcome with a drastic or dramatically uncomfortable feeling or a circumstance or an activity that we avoid facing or engaging in at all costs to the extent that it creates enormous difficulties. For years as a professional, I feared those around me would discover that I am dyslexic. I learned that dyslexia for me was actually a 'gift' which has literally sharpened and elevated ways in which I communicate, process information, learn, prepare myself for public speaking engagements and presentations, create and have trained myself to function. For years however in silence, I was self-conscious, even ashamed at times after discovering my learning disability that would actually connect unconnected dots for me dating back to elementary school. I can remember working on my homework at the dining room table as a child with my grandfather who had the most perfect and regal penmanship ever, looked over at me and said – "boy, you write like somebody's joking you!" (The funny thing is, after all those years I still do which is why I am a little nervous about any future book signings).

Nonetheless, imagine feeling out of fear of disclosure, having to mask my secret for instance, when presenting and reading lengthy proclamations in front of hundreds of people, elected officials and dignitaries on behalf of Ohio's former

Governor Ted Strickland in my role then as Community Outreach Coordinator in the Cleveland Regional Office of the Governor. Sometimes I would actually commit to memory entire pre-written presentations and proclamations for fear of mispronouncing a word or misreading a sentence as words on a page at times appear to rearrange themselves in front of my very eyes. Can you imagine feeling fearful and anxious while reading from a podium in a room filled with community leaders, politicians and the media and you mispronounce a word that's not even on the page as if your brain briefly, but unbeknownst to others, goes on automatic pilot?

As I look to my furthest and most vivid memory as a child, I clearly recall being afraid of the dark and those sounds that would go bump in the night. I lived in an older home, a side-by-side duplex on Churchill Avenue in the Glenville area of Cleveland. My bedroom was at the top of the stairs, while my grandparents' bedroom was on the first floor. Oh, how I remember fighting sleep and putting off going to bed as long as I could, then instructing my grandfather to turn off the light from the bottom of the stairs once I'd gone to sleep. A nightlight just wouldn't do. As if it was yesterday, I can hear the light switch click and see the darkness envelop my room as I alert my grandfather, "I'm not asleep yet!" It wasn't the darkness that was frightening to me as much as it was the sounds of the wind blowing the mulberry tree against the back of the house, the sounds I thought I heard coming from behind the attic door just down the hallway, and the pictures on my wall that I would take down as they appeared to be staring at me ever so deviously. Be that as it may, that was my fear as a child, but it was also my reality.

Nearly forty-five years later (it is fair to say for the record and to my 2 six-year-old grandsons, that I am not afraid of the dark anymore, although I do still close my bedroom closet door before going to sleep since the clothes hanging on the rack sometimes still look like people standing in the closet), I confronted another lifelong fear and apprehension. I could not swim, and the sheer thought of being underwater after a traumatic near drowning incident when I was 13…well, let's just say I'd rather give myself a root canal. Imagine being an adolescent on a hot summer day, watching your friends at the community swimming pool splashing around, going down the slide, and leaping off the diving board. I can still see their smiling faces and hear their laughter from all the fun they were having, while I sat on the side of the pool with a "no, not me" look on my face.

Even as an adult, I watched my young children swim like Flipper the dolphin in the pool on the grounds of our apartment complex and heard the countless requests: "Daddy, come get in the pool." Of course, my patented, countless response was simply, "Nope!" So, prior to the release of this book, I finally registered for adult swimming lessons at the neighborhood YMCA in Warrensville Heights, Ohio. I am facing my fear of swimming head on, learning the correct techniques, but above all I have changed my approach and mindset in a way that has been transformative in other aspects of my life.

I decided to face and replace my fear of water with faith as I seek the face of God. You may be asking yourself what any of this has to do with learning how to swim for the first time as a nearly fifty-year-old man. What this says to me is, despite how anxious, uncomfortable, afraid, nervous, unsure, unconfident, and fearful I allowed myself to become regarding swimming, if God is with me, what reason do I have to be afraid? I simply needed to activate my faith to its highest degree and believe that He could, not only remove my fears but that I would not be alone as He would be in my midst. So in taking my first Saturday swimming lesson at the Y in March of 2015, in actuality I was seeking God's face and inviting His presence as I climbed down the ladder into the swimming pool. At that point, it did not matter that I was in only four feet of water, nor did it matter that I could see what appeared to be eight-year-olds swimming like fish at the deep end of the pool. All that mattered to me was that I had gathered enough faith to overcome a lifelong fear and barrier and believed that not only was I in the hands of a capable swim instructor but in the omnipresence of an awesome, mighty, and all-capable God.

I'm not sure what your fear may be today. It could be delivering a presentation at a meeting for work, taking a flight, or submerging your head underwater while learning how to swim for the first time. Just know that God already knows your fears, but your faith and trust in Him are what help to remove them. Seek His face, which means seek and invite His presence. Then know, just at that very moment of facing what has been difficult for you to face, that this is the same God who locked the lions' jaws while Daniel stood in the den. This is the same God who raised Lazarus from the grave. And this is the same God who will stand with you and stand in the gap for you as you face and overcome whichever fear or obstacle you may have.

I do not know when I will be diving off anyone's diving board into the swimming pool. But I do know that whenever that day comes, God will be with me. Therefore, I will not be afraid.

Thirteen

When the Weight Gets Too Heavy

*I*f you have ever lifted free weights—especially bench pressed—or know someone who has, you may be able to identify with this message. Visualize yourself or someone else trying to get those last few repetitions while on the workout bench. No matter how strong, determined, well trained, prepared, or in good shape you are, it still helps to have a spotter over or with you in the gym. It helps to have a workout partner there to push you, motivate you, encourage you, and even guide the weight upward when you need it at just the right moment. That person also serves as a sense of security and prevents the weight from falling back on you if your arms begin to weaken or give out. Sometimes just knowing that the spotter is there can be all the confidence you need to make that final push to completion or to reach your full potential or goal. I have lifted a heavier weight with confidence, thinking that the spotter was helping me. I didn't know it was me pushing all alone, but I thought I was pushing with the spotter as my guide and helper. There comes a time, however, after you have done all you can with the abilities, strength, determination, preparation, technique, and willpower you have, when the weight gets too heavy to bear or handle. Then you say to the spotter, "Take it." In my experience with weightlifting (not to say that I am an authority or expert in the gym), the spotter usually responds, "I got it," or "I got you." He or she may not utter a word, but in the nick of time, when there is a sign of struggle, the spotter takes the weight from you so that you don't injure yourself.

When it comes to the weights in my life and the weights of this world, my daily prayer is, "Lord, please guide me, strengthen me," or "Lord, please take this weight from me as I can't handle it alone." I am so glad that God is my spotter and is always there with me throughout all my struggles and heavy lifting. He knows my limits, strengths, weaknesses, and what I can bear. Most of all, when the weight gets too heavy for me to lift, His love still lifts me. What a blessed assurance and what a joy divine to know that there is nothing too heavy for God to lift off you. If you find yourself in a situation where the burden is too heavy to bear and the pressure and weight that you face are more than you can lift off of you, know with all certainty that God is there with you as your spotter. He can take the weight from you and be your guide as His yoke is easy, and His burden is light.

FOURTEEN

Can You Keep a Secret?

I probably shouldn't say this, but I am about to give away a million-...no, a billion-...no, a trillion-... nope, a quintillion-dollar secret, so listen closely. If you are seriously involved with someone—be it a significant other, a business partner, a collaborator, someone with whom you're undergoing a merger, a person under whose faith teachings you are learning within a ministry, an elected official you are supporting, or someone with whom you are considering a critical union or agreement—remember this: if you either don't or can't trust that individual entirely and unconditionally, you are probably with the wrong person at the wrong place or in the wrong situation.

But, shhhh...don't tell anyone I told you. Please trust your judgment and "be wise as serpents" today. (Matthew 10:16).

Then let God be your guide and pray for discernment, because if something or some situation doesn't feel right then it's probably not right and needs serious and wise reevaluation, counsel, or intervention. The sixth sense you feel within your spirit but can't quite put your finger on could very well be the Holy Spirit inside you, sounding an alarm, especially if at the center of your concern, hesitation, or what is giving you pause in your situation is trust. God not only opens doors, opens the windows of heaven, and pours out blessings you won't have room enough to receive; He also opens eyes.

FIFTEEN

Your Steps Are Ordered

Never give up on your journey or your dreams when you know that your steps are ordered, and the favor of God is with you. There may be thorns and snares along the way with doubters and distractions, hurdles and hidden setbacks, but faith is the victory that overcomes the world. Failure is not an option when your Father in heaven created and is the author of the entire universe. Yes, you just may have the perfect portfolio, the perfect résumé, and impeccable credentials; you may know all the right people in all the right places, but know that your steps are ordered by an all-perfect God, who has a purpose for your life that just may differ from the plan you have set forth. It is wise to be prepared and pursue excellence, but true wisdom is knowing that your steps were ordered before the earth was even formed.

Sixteen

His Healing Hands Extended

I can attest firsthand to the healing power of God. It was in April of 2013 when I had a major procedure performed to restore sight in one of my eyes after suffering a detached retina while driving. The doctor stated that the procedure I would undergo has a fifty-fifty chance of success. With 90 percent of my vision gone, it was as if a black curtain had eventually lowered over my left eye, and I barely saw my feet in front of me. I originally panicked and feared the worst, but I prayed without ceasing and did not lose faith.

The eye specialist performed a successful emergency procedure. The recovery was intense and grueling as it required me to hang inverted over the side of the bed, suspended face down with only my elbows and a pillow supporting me for twenty hours a day over ten consecutive days. I followed the doctor's instructions and had the attentive aid of my caring girlfriend, who was at my side, but, more importantly, I was comforted by my faith that God, and God alone, would have the final say on the restoration of my sight. I've since fully recovered with minimum aftereffects but with maximum revival of my faith and belief in the amazing power of God. For me, that experience was a reminder of His goodness, mercy, grace, and favor: "for by His stripes, we are healed." (Isaiah 53:5).

If you or someone close to you is faced with a trying medical circumstance, procedure, affliction, or condition, I pray that the Lord guides the hands of the medical professionals as God stands in the midst, extending His healing hands toward you.

SEVENTEEN

You Do the Math

Having a life problem you can't solve? Here's a possible answer: subtract yourself; add God to the equation; let there be no division between you; locate the common denominator; move the decimal points until they align with God's will; factor in His sufficient grace and favor to the infinite power; then watch as the desires of your heart are multiplied. Anything less than would be equal to only a fraction of a solution. Now, you do the math!

EIGHTEEN

Easier Said Than Done

There may come a day when you feel that you are carrying the weight of the world on your shoulders. You hear silence while in search of solutions to your situation, and though the sun is shining, you feel caught in a thunderstorm on your side of the street.

On days like this, getting up, getting out, and getting through your daily routine are easier said than done. In times like these, we often focus on our needs when this is when we may need to focus on the needs of someone else who draws strength from us, even in our weakened states. There is someone—maybe a significant other, a child, a coworker, a classmate, a social media friend/connection, a student, or someone within your institution of faith—who, possibly unbeknown to you during your trial, is being uplifted and encouraged simply because you refuse to give up, give in, or be defeated or depleted by your circumstance.

God may have placed this individual or individuals along your path to draw from your inner strength, faith, and determination, even if you are feeling not at your best. What they may not know is where your help and strength are coming from. Through your circumstance, through your unwavering, unshakable, and unmovable faith, you may be the vessel that leads them to Christ. Even in that very moment when you are wondering how you are going to carry on, through self-determination, perseverance, faithfulness, and relentless effort, God makes a way out of no way.

With His love and favor, He works through you, works on you, and works to prepare you for your breakthrough all while sustaining someone else who is being encouraged by you. It's so amazing that what seems hard and hopeless to us is easy and effortless to God.

So just when your heart is heaviest, the deals appear to have folded, your deliverance seems delayed, or your feet are racing in one direction when the opportunity appears to be going in the other, that is when you press on even harder. This is when you humble yourself before God, thanking Him for what He has already done, because you are not just pressing on for yourself but for someone else who is standing on your shoulders, borrowing from your strength and endurance. While that someone is standing on your shoulders or leaning on your side for support as a result of your faith, just know that you are standing on God's shoulders, and He is in control.

Nineteen

The Past Is Important

What history has taught us and where your personal experiences have brought you from are important. All that we have gone through, including the trials and travails of others around us and before us, helps to contribute to our state of consciousness and awareness. However, the pains of the past should not be a license or permission to not progress or prevail today. But the past should be the lesson and launching pad to perseverance and promise—and to where God is positioning you to be.

TWENTY

Did You Forget?

Upon starting each day, we seldom forget to check the weather forecast before leaving the house. We seldom forget to check our calendars or agendas for the day. We seldom forget to check our email, text, or voicemail messages. And we seldom forget to make sure that our cellphones are charged or the charger is nearby. But too often we forget to thank God for starting each day. Thank you, God, for allowing me to see another day and for starting me on my way.

TWENTY-ONE

From Stumbling Block to Stepping Stone

Somebody somewhere needs to hear this loud and clear today and every day: Don't quit! Don't give up! Keep the faith! You're almost there, and God's favor is upon you! I tell myself this even when no one else is around. When you are in that quiet place alone with your thoughts is sometimes when you most need to hear such words of encouragement reverberate within your spirit and inner being. These words may be helpful to someone who has tried again and again in pursuit of his or her dream or who may have poured or sacrificed all of his or her abilities, time, treasure, and resources into preparation for achieving something great. Someone else may be knocking on a door to unlock the barriers in a broken relationship within their immediate, extended, or blended family.

Maybe it's the relationship with your spouse or significant other, where you once followed your heart but then found yourself unable to overcome or work through mounting obstacles, conflict, or differences, or maybe the love you once felt, expressed or shared just isn't there anymore. You may have reached a crossroad in that relationship where that person was once the apple of your eye, but now you are not treating each other with love and respect. Your heart aches from the conflict, and then distance separates you. There comes a pivotal moment when you have done all you can do or know how to do, and you are ready to throw in the towel. You are poor in spirit, and the Goliaths in your life appear to be lined up against you. This is when you know you are approaching a breakthrough, and the fruit of your labor, for which you worked hard and that you so diligently and faithfully pursued, is at hand. So let no outside influences, distractions, negativity, or insensitivity sidetrack you from what is in your grasp or has been divinely set aside for you.

The test through which you are going will no doubt be your testimony once you get through it. What appears to be a stumbling block or unforeseen setback may actually be a stepping stone or your comeback in disguise. You will not only emerge from your struggle with a renewed sense of purpose but as an inspiration to others during *their* stormy seasons. We all have assignments while here on earth that go far beyond our aspirations involving careers, people, places, and things. At some point, our personal pursuits should align with God's purpose for our lives. This is what makes us complete and is the real definition of what it means to be successful. Success is not simply measured by the size of our homes, cars, credentials, and bank accounts or by our ability to maintain and survive. Success is also measured by the lives you have been able to successfully touch, impact, and stand in the gap for with the abilities, strengths, gifts, and talents God gave you.

Do not be weary in well-doing. I can speak from personal experience, and I am sure you can too. I remember leaving my hometown of Cleveland, Ohio, to join my love interest in the San Francisco Bay Area. *(By the way, congratulations to the Golden State Warriors on winning the 2015 NBA Finals. Yes, I am a die-hard Cleveland Cavaliers fan, but attended a few Warrior games with my Students of Promise while living in the Bay Area and followed them regularly).* She had relocated as a result of a prestigious promotion, career opportunities, and her love for the beautiful city of St. Francis. I relocated as a result of my love for her, the beautiful woman I was hoping to make my wife. So beautiful, that for me it was love at first sight as everyone in the room seemed to disappear the moment I saw her at a social gathering near Case Western Reserve University one evening. We would then date each other for nearly the next 7 years. At the time, I thought we were very much in love, and I had little doubt that she and I were the perfect pair. So I dropped everything, took a leap of faith, and headed westward. While I was in Cleveland, my career was on the rise as a public servant in the administration of the office of the County Executive in Cuyahoga County.

I was ultimately appointed as one of the Special Assistants to the County Executive as well as the first legislative liaison to the first Cuyahoga County Council under the new charter government. I had become increasingly active in social, political, and educational issues over the years and was regarded as a community-minded advocate by my peers and many professionals in Greater Cleveland

I know now, however, that God had another plan for me in San Francisco quite different from why I chose to move there. Through His favor, I was able to launch a youth initiative *(Students of Promise)*, to address the achievement gap within the San Francisco Unified School District that would impact the lives of many students and their families.

The highlight of my few years in the Bay Area included producing and directing a documentary about the one hundred and sixtieth anniversary of Third Baptist Church, the oldest African-American faith institution west of the Rockies. I was honored to interview the legendary actor and activist Danny Glover for the documentary, which was also a priceless moment I would have never dreamed of experiencing while in Cleveland. I had the privilege to work closely with and be mentored by the Reverend Dr. Amos C. Brown, pastor of Third Baptist Church in San Francisco and president of the San Francisco NAACP, among other national accolades. Dr. Brown was also mentored by the late Medgar Evers and was one of eight students in a course taught by Dr. Martin Luther King Jr. at Morehouse College in Atlanta. Rev. Brown and his wife, First Lady Jane Brown, reminded me so much of my grandparents that I have no doubt that God placed me in their path to shepherd me with their love, acceptance, wisdom, and wise counsel while I was in the Bay Area.

I also had the pleasure of meeting and working with some of the most amazing students, teachers, and staff at Dr. Martin Luther King Jr. Academic Middle School in San Francisco while leading an effort that flew seventeen students to Morehouse College in Atlanta to witness President Barack Obama deliver the commencement address. Yes, there were moments when I stumbled both personally and professionally while living in the Bay Area. But in the final analysis, taking that leap of faith was ultimately a stepping stone that would reveal to me my true purpose as an advocate, administrator, and change agent in the lives of youth at risk. I state these various experiences along my journey not to focus on what Bob has done, but to magnify what God has done!

My relocation, after being well established in my hometown, had its share of hurdles, ups, and downs. There were several occasions when I would second guess my decisions and my abilities as well as my relationship, but, through it all, I followed my heart once again—this time in prayer. I have no regrets about taking that leap of faith or leaving Cleveland to be with the love and heart I moved to California to join. God, however, had another plan for me. He opened even wider doors upon my return to Cleveland. The initial doors opened were those of my dear friend Cedric Sims, who designed the cover of my book, and his lovely wife, Helen. They opened their home to me for a couple weeks since my new apartment was not quite ready to move into upon my return to the Cleveland area. I was rooming in a costly extended-stay hotel; they would have no part of that and extended an invitation for me to stay with them until my apartment was finished.

I now direct a major youth initiative in Cuyahoga County aimed at closing the achievement gap and increasing the high school graduation rate. Since my return to Cleveland, I am much wiser, more humble, and more purpose-driven than I was before I'd left.

So I say with conviction: Be encouraged; never quit or give up. Follow your heart but first ask God to guide it and be in the midst of all you do. Keep the faith as God's favor will follow you wherever you may go, and His will shall be done on earth as it is in heaven. What may appear to be a rough road or stumbling blocks along your path may very well be a stepping stone in disguise. You may not realize it at the time, but God may have already decided, worked it out, and delivered you into His perfect plan and purpose for your life.

Twenty-Two

Somebody Prayed for You

I say to any and all who may be in the midst of a personal or professional turning point or uncertainty: your hard work, dedication, and faithfulness, despite any odds or obstacles, will pay off. Nothing is greater than the power of prayer. It works as you wait for God's answer, favor, outcome, or deliverance. I am also grateful for those who prayed over me and for me from the very beginning and throughout my life. I have no doubt in my mind that my great-grandmother and others in the small town of Lake Village, Arkansas, where I was born, prayed over me shortly after I came into the world, prayers that God Almighty is still honoring today.

I make it a point to do the same each night, as I am at the fifty-year milestone, to call out each of my children's and grandchildren's names to the Lord in prayer. First is my oldest son, Timothy, who is a hard-working father who now has the awesome responsibility of raising his son without his son's mother, who passed away suddenly at the tender age of 28. My oldest daughter, Kyerra, is a strong and loving mother, studying to be an RN and is a veteran of both the Iraq and Afghanistan wars serving her country honorably. I would pray tirelessly for her safe return during her deployments overseas. My middle son, Chris, now Attorney at Law, who passed the Georgia Bar Exam on his first attempt fresh out of Law School and I have no doubt is destined to be a world changer. My youngest daughter, Jasmine whom also received her Master's Degree in Education, through her spiritual transformation and faith walk, inspired the title of this book. I had already selected a title for the book but after reading a draft copy and hearing the song, she suggested and I agreed the book should be appropriately titled "What God Has Done". My youngest namesake, Lil Bob, is the apple of my eye and a brilliant young man excelling in high school. He aspires to attend The Ohio State University, following in the footsteps of three of his older siblings in which I am very proud. As my grandparents prayed for me, I call the names of my two grandsons Chase and Parris to the Lord as "GrandBobby" loves them so. We must go to God in prayer not only to help us be the best we can be for our children, grandchildren and family members, but to ask God to show mercy and camp His angels around them, a prayer I know He hears, honors and answers according to His will.

Yes, we prepare ourselves to get where we are going in a number of traditional ways: educationally, professionally, and through our contacts, associations, relationships, and experiences. Imagine how far God will take you when you simply stay grounded, help others, become better stewards, and recognize, as I have come to learn, where we would be had not somebody prayed for us.

Mama Dean, as we called my great-grandmother in Arkansas, passed away in 1977, when I was twelve years old. As a preteen, it was my first time experiencing death and being confronted with such sadness, grief, loss, and pain. I loved her so. I remember calling her on the phone and playing her favorite song, "Amazing Grace," on the piano when I was about nine years old. She was born in 1897, and I know that her prayers over me and her family, from her lips to God's ear, still echo today in the hallways and mansions throughout heaven. Thank you to so many who, I have no doubt, prayed for me.

Twenty-Three

Hurry, Run for Your Life into God's Awaiting, Outstretched Arms!

*I*f you're anything like me, your nightly dreams can be very vivid, illuminating, revealing, and, at times, troubling. For as long as I can remember, my dreams have been so realistic and lifelike that I actually thought I was awake in some of them. I've heard music and entire songs in my sleep so clearly that I could remember the song when I woke up from the dream. I have even played a song or melody on the piano that I had never heard before but remembered from a dream as an original composition. (I'm still waiting to dream a song like "Ribbon in the Sky" or "Don't Worry, Be Happy"!) I will never forget a dream I had when my late grandfather and late younger brother, who passed away only two months apart in 1992, appeared to me. The dream was the most realistic, dynamic, and peaceful experience I've ever had. In this dream, which was not long after my grandfather's homegoing celebration, he and my younger brother hovered outside my bedroom window, surrounded by swirling wind and an orange and yellow glowing light. They both assured me they were okay and at peace and told me to be strong for the family. What I will never forget about the dream is that some of the orange and yellow glow fell upon me while I was in my bed, leaving me with a euphoric sensation that words cannot describe. Another memorable and emotional dream I had years later included a walk down the halls of my high school while in conversation with my biological father, who I never knew; he passed away when I was ten years old. When a sound awakened me from that dream, I actually shed a few tears in frustration and sadness since, in this dream, my biological father and I had started to have a conversation that would have answered a list of questions I had, and still have, that only he could answer.

This passage is not about Bob Ivory's dream-world experiences since all of us dream nightly, although we all may not remember the dreams, according to the experts. Nonetheless, I would like to share with you a dream I had after this book was completed and submitted for final edits. I felt led to include this passage because it may be of encouragement to or have an impact on someone at a critical point in his or her life. In addition to that, it was placed on my heart to share for a reason.

I titled this chapter of the book "Hurry, Run for Your Life into God's Awaiting, Outstretched Arms" because that was the overarching message of the dream—not in a horrific sense, because it was not a nightmare, but in a spiritual context as if I were on the receiving end of divine instruction. My interpretation of this dream left me in such deep thought and was so spiritually uplifting that I had to include my experience in this book before its final edit for publishing. I don't think it is a coincidence or insignificant that I had this dream on New Year's Day. This was symbolic for me as a new beginning and as turning the page to a new chapter in my life.

In this dream, there was an assertive yet surreal voice that spoke to me about a spiritual warfare taking place within, as if to be alerting me, awakening me, protecting me, preparing me, and advising me. I identified this voice as one of divine authority, majesty, and firmness, but it spoke with great compassion, concern, and reassurance.

In essence, this dream pointed out to me that I was in the midst of a series of internal struggles or battles wherein I was confronted with choices, tests, temptations, and distractions. At the same time, I was aware that I was seeking a closer walk with God and was approaching a breakthrough moment in many aspects of my life. The "hurry, run for your life" theme suggests to me that I should resist, retreat, and feverishly head in the opposite direction of anything that may be contrary to the breakthrough and blessing that

God Himself is preparing to release. This notion was not limited to physically running for my life inasmuch as it was a spiritual and conscious awakening instructing me to seek and find the will of God for my life in the midst of external and/or self-imposed elements that could be blocking my blessings.

I began to analyze this dream in more detail and interpret it in a variety of ways. Could this dream mean I should take a closer look at choices and decisions I was making or would soon make? Were my priorities in place, or was I putting too much emphasis on some aspects of my life and not enough on others? Was I just merely *talking* about a healthier lifestyle, healthy eating habits, diet, and exercise, or was I putting words into action by taking better care of my body as a holy temple. (Not to digress, but please understand that my eating habits have gone from devouring 3 to 4 Cleveland style Polish Boy's and a 2-liter of Tahitian Treat a week, to apple cider, fresh salads, nuts and berries as my treats of choice!) My dream made me question if there were any distractions that would take me off the path that God would have me travel versus where I wanted to venture out to on my own for personal reasons and motivations. Could my sense of feeling lonely and void of companionship or a reciprocating love interest be consuming me as opposed to allowing God to work out present or future relationships as He worked on me, mind, body, and spirit? Most of all, were there any old wounds, unresolved issues, hurts, ways, thought patterns, thinking errors, or behaviors that I might succumb to if I didn't consciously remain focused, lean forward, and pursue God's way instead of Bob's way?

I took the meaning of "run for your life" to represent fleeing—at all costs and at top speed—distractions, negative thoughts and impulses, patterns of behaviors, and even people, places, and things that may be coming between me and the spiritual walk I desire to have. I do not mean this in an extreme, radical, or "holier than thou" sense nor by judging others since we do not know the shoes someone else may walk in as we all fall short of the glory of God. However, I wanted to consciously begin to flee poor choices, patterns of behavior, and temptations that I can admit have been personal stumbling blocks— even spiked speed bumps—along the road of my life.

In this dream, I was given no clear examples or specifics as to what these elements or areas in my life may be, but as I looked inside myself and around me, I knew exactly what they were. It would require me to look at recent choices I had made, actions I had taken in certain situations, temptations, moments of weakness, my stewardship, matters of the heart, and ways in which I had been communicating with people closest to me. Once I took this internal and personal inventory and reflected on these areas, I was to address any and every scenario or action that may have been detrimental to or stunting my spiritual growth. This would all be in preparation for what God would have in store for my life.

Well, some may say this is no real news flash or epiphany since we all know to run from, turn away from, or distance ourselves from what is not good for us, to resist temptation, and to make wise choices. Because this message came to me in a dream minus the distractions and impulses of day-to-day living, I felt there was a deeper context, even concern, for the direction of my life, physically, spiritually, and emotionally. I'm sure many of you can relate to this and are devout believers that God wants to do something incredible in your life that equates you to your purpose and desires of your heart as He prepares to bless you according to His will and riches. At the same time, you may be doing something that is contrary to how He wants to bless you, even if it is making poor choices, being involved in a negative cycle that is spinning out of control, making ill-advised decisions, being a poor steward, or succumbing to temptation, bad influences, and the pressures of this world. Of course, none of us is perfect or without stain, sin, or blemish, but if you are anything like me, when you know better, you should do better.

This brings me to the conclusion that a spiritual warfare and inner struggle can exist and persist within us. I interpreted my dream to also mean that I should hold myself more accountable for and aware of my surroundings, reevaluate my choices, become more God-centered, and raise expectations in all that I do. I don't think I had to be in a deep sleep to identify with the message of my dream. I am humbled by the fact that I heard this voice loud and clear, minus the stimuli and distractions each day brings, to the point that I was moved to take heed, self-inventory, and meaningful action.

Keep in mind that there is a distinct difference between hearing a voice of reason and actually identifying with it, listening, and discerning what the voice is really saying. We may hear the voice of reason all the time, either internally or externally. The question that should give us all pause is: are we listening or paying critical attention to the message behind the words that the voice is saying? Equally important, are we asking ourselves from where the voice behind the message is coming? Is the message aligned with God's holy word, book, chapter, and verse? Is the message simply saying what we want to hear while filtering out what we don't want to hear or face? Is the message evidence-based in spirituality, or does it have a worldly, humanistic, feel-good connotation? This is the beginning of discernment.

All I could think about once I was awakened from this dream was that I did not want to miss out on any blessing that God may be preparing to open up His window and pour out for me. We can conceive of getting promotions in our jobs, purchasing new homes, being blessed with the birth of a child, or receiving whatever you would consider to bring you great joy, fulfillment, accomplishment, and happiness. But can you truly conceive of, imagine, or wrap your mind around God pouring out a blessing that you won't have room enough to receive? Now that is something I do not want to miss! Neither do I want to knowingly continue to place myself at risk by ignoring the message or sign from this dream.

In hopes that it may resonate with some aspect of your life, I will share with you that this dream appeared so real and relative to my life that I could feel the spirit of the Lord in the room. I immediately and reverently humbled myself before Him and gave thanks in advance, and I asked Him to deliver me from all with which I may be struggling and battling. During this quiet moment, I prayed that God would remove, according to His will, anything from within me or around me that is hindering me from walking in His fullness and becoming the true child of God that He would have us all be.

So I think it is appropriate to describe my dream as a "run for your life" encounter since spiritual warfare is real and nothing to ignore. There is truly a battle for our very lives, mentally, emotionally, spiritually, and physically. There are some battles that I know we must give to God. Those notwithstanding, there are areas in our lives where we have to stand firm; we must confront, process, resist, seek wise counsel on, and ultimately resolve these issues. This is why we must pray for and be an inspiration to each other. As believers, we must be strong when someone may be weak and have unwavering faith when someone else may need to draw from our faith.

What is the "hurry, run for your life" situation with which you are faced today? Are there any reoccurring indicators, alerts, or flashing red lights that you have been ignoring in one or more areas of your life? Have you minimized or justified things that are actually signs and signals indicating that you are in over your head in a situation and need the guidance of or an intercession from God and His holy word? Are there any areas in which you need to engage someone—not just someone to side with you or tell you what you want to hear but someone who you know has your best interest at heart and has a strong, spirit-filled relationship with God him- or herself?

If you are at a defining moment in your life, as I was at the time of this dream, hurry! Run for your life into the awaiting, outstretched arms of God! There's nothing He can't do or see you through as He came not only for you to have life but to have it more abundantly.

Twenty-Four

Short Messages on Which to Meditate

(Share one each day with someone you care about.)

You are all the medicine someone needs today. Fill his or her prescription with your sincerity and kindness. Then give him or her a double dose of your loving and caring heart.

We must first be able to meet our young people where they are in order to help bring them to where they need to be.

Until you clearly understand your true worth and value, someone will always be nearby to define them for you.

When you love what you do, your work is like eating your favorite ice cream all day long, never getting sick, and never gaining a pound. Everything in moderation, but a labor of love needs very little.

Seeking wealth and prosperity is one thing, but if your success has to come at the expense of someone else, that's a success you can't afford to have.

Your truth and *the* truth are two different and separate realities. Wisdom is understanding the difference between the two.

Hold on to your faith. It's going to be okay, because He's still up there watching over you.

I find no greater charge, choice, or challenge than taking the gifts and abilities that God has given us and trying to make this world a better place with them.

It's sometimes easy to think that the grass is greener on the other side—until reality sets in, and you realize that unwatered grass turns brown too.

When you are not happy, it is hard to bring happiness to someone else. However, it's no one's responsibility to *make* you happy; true happiness begins within from knowing that you are a child of God.

Sometimes success can be measured by what you were willing to do with the abilities God gave you when the next person was not.

Water your dreams with determination, diligence, desire, and devotion and watch them grow into a forest of possibilities that replenish themselves.

Let nothing, no one, or no circumstance steer you off the course or path that God has already placed you upon and predestined for you.

Facing a tough or life-altering decision or transition? Don't just sit on the shore, watching the waves roll in. Once your destiny is in view, you may have to swim out to meet it despite the water tread or the combination of strokes to stay afloat. What God has for you is for you, and it was determined before the earth was even formed. God must be in the decision and the equation as the inspiration and the motivation; anything else will produce the illusion of success built on an undercurrent of disappointment.

Before there was typing, texting, tweeting, and high tech, there was talking, quality time, togetherness, and high touch.

What a joy it is to wake up to another day filled with opportunities, expectations, avenues, and options. As long as you have air to breathe and are allowed another day, you can not only pursue happiness but be utilized as an active participant in God's purpose for your life.

This may be the day your miracle comes looking for you. Your hard work, prayers, patience, and faith deliver and unleash what God has set aside just for you all along.

The stumbling blocks on the pathway to what *you* want to do may be the very stepping stones to where *God* wants to elevate you to new heights that you cannot even imagine.

Hard work, preparation, determination, God's plan for your life, and God's favor on your life are the perfect recipe for success.

I am sure that one-a-day vitamins are healthy, but several-times-a-day acts of kindness, consideration, and affection will not only help you but will help someone else be healthier too.

You develop a greater appreciation of God's greatness when you digest these facts:

- One apple may produce seven apple seeds.
- One apple tree is produced from just one apple seed.
- Four hundred apples are produced from just one apple tree.

If an apple seed is planted, watered, provided with sunlight, and nurtured in fertile ground under the right conditions, it can produce endless fruit. Then imagine the possibilities of what can be produced when the seeds of love and compassion are planted and nurtured within us.

The Transference of Emotions: Be careful not to transfer unresolved feelings or emotions from one relationship with a previous significant other to another. This would be like attempting to transfer a permanent tattoo from one arm to the next as if it were drawn with an erasable or washable marker. Follow your heart, but proceed with caution. You may always cherish fond memories from past encounters, but you cannot truly give your heart to another, when you know yourself your heart truly still belongs to someone else.

Life starting to veer off course? You may want to take your foot off the accelerator, get out of the fast lane, and give God the wheel. While He steers you to safety and gets you back on track, turn your owner's manual to Proverbs 3:6, where it reads: "In all your ways acknowledge Him, and He shall direct your path." Consider this your midweek tune-up!

Your toil, your time, your trials, your tenacity, and your tests will all be worth it in the end. Be encouraged, stay focused, and trust God. Change is coming.

To be 'happy' or experience happiness is something we all strive for. To have or be filled with 'joy' is clearly a separate end-goal. Joy is beyond a feeling that may come or go. It needs no stimulation, human participation nor activation. Joy is a state of mind, a total existence and a holistic experience and acknowledgement. It graciously embraces and dwells within our spirit and surrounds us at the highest level of peace without conditions. In a world that can be cold, cruel, and chaotic at times, it's sometimes hard to identify with the essence of 'joy' therefore resolving to be 'happy' in its place. Happy is a good thing, however 'joy' is a God thing. Just knowing that no matter what the situation over the years God has seen and brought you through and will continue to do is unthinkable joy within itself. So in all you acquire and in all you do today as time marches on, may you have and find 'joy' and an abundance of it. Joy is not hard to find as God is here, there and everywhere.

When you have compatibility and like-mindedness even in rough times, you can find smooth endings, but when you are incompatible, heading in opposite directions, driven by conflicting values, and viewing life through separate and unequal lenses, it may make for long days, sleepless nights, and rough roads ahead. Whenever you find common and solid ground with a firm foundation anchored in the Lord, and equal footing to build upon, you've found a good thing.

No matter how high the hurdle, obstacle, distraction or challenge, it is important to remain diligent, focused and grounded as you persevere. Even in cases when you may be your own hindrance or barrier, one must still reach deep inside seek God's guidance, purpose and His perfect will for your life. Press on and persevere until you've established solid footing and know that through God's amazing grace, victory is already won.

TWENTY-FIVE

Words with a Message from My Music

Sound, rhythm, harmony, and melody embody your innermost feelings and thoughts and your outwardly displayed actions and emotions. In essence, this is what a song is to me. Although it presents itself and reaches us in various formats, genres, tempos, arrangements, instrumentation, and voices, inspired and captured from the imagination and experiences of the writer, a song and its music continue to be a universal language.

What God Has Done is my first book, but I have written a multitude of songs since high school. While growing up, I spent a lot of time alone. In addition to learning to play the piano at an early age, I also discovered how to write down my thoughts and set them to music simultaneously. Please allow me to share a few of those thoughts and reflective moments that I have written out over the years as you meditate on the lyrics minus sound, rhythm, timbre, melody, and harmony. These are simply words of inspiration that complement this book and were placed on my heart as a result of a variety of experiences and expressions. I hope that my song lyrics, inspired by familiar journeys and themes, speak to your heart, mind, and soul.

I am confident that you will find some lyric, verse, or phrase with which you will identify. Some of the songs I've selected to share were written at turning points in my life with tears flowing, others with unthinkable joy and laughter. I felt it important to share with you a brief backdrop or short narrative of what inspired each song in order to place the lyrics into the right contexts. I encourage you to see what kind of journey my songs may take you on based on your personal experiences, faith, relationships, and emotions. I would also like to invite you to download each inspirational song I've shared at www.bobivory.com or at Amazon.com so that you may hear and experience the actual musical recordings and arrangements. Follow along with the lyrics that were placed on my heart to share. Be encouraged...and enjoy!

"What God Has Done"

I wrote the song "What God Has Done" in 1997 at a tumultuous time in my life, when my mindset and emotions were literally all over the place. If not for God undergirding me, the friendship and faithfulness of the Stringer family in Cleveland, and my best friend since college, Ron Woodson, I'm not sure how I would have made it through that difficult period of my life. I was working as a juvenile correctional officer at Cuyahoga Hills Boys School outside of Cleveland at the time. I had been a State of Ohio employee for about eleven consecutive years. I was also heavily involved in pursuing a career in music as a songwriter and producer with a growing catalogue of original material, mainly R&B. I wrote and recorded music daily while having the privilege of collaborating and working with some of the best vocalists, musicians, producers, studios, and songwriters in the Cleveland area. I signed a contract with a major management company out of Atlanta and Nashville that had all the right connections, credentials, successes, industry savvy, and insidership.

I felt that after years of writing and recording, I was finally about to really make it and that my music career was in capable hands. I had come close a few times with several local recording projects and artists in the past, but nothing compared to the energy that was surrounding the music I was writing then and the level of representation I had. I was recording all the time, flying here and there to various studios in different cities, and getting rave reviews for my unique and signature writing style, sound, and original songs.

As far as my personal life was concerned, I was engaged to be married to a beautiful young lady, and I felt as if I were on top of the world. That is, until my world began to collapse and tumble and crumble around me, piece by piece.

As I was anticipating a major six-figure publishing, production, and endorsement deal signing, negotiated by the management team and entertainment attorney I was assigned to, the deals all fell through and were no longer on the table (at least the deals that were pertaining to me). I had put in so much time, sacrifice, and effort, musically and creatively, to the point that I just knew, as a songwriter, I was well on my way to becoming the next Babyface. The disappointment from this letdown left me extremely depressed, miserable, and withdrawn as well as frustrated, hurt, and angry.

Also, around that same time period, my engagement was called off a week before the wedding was to take place. This was devastating and heartbreaking for me, to say the least. I honestly felt that we were the perfect pair. (She was "my idea" of the perfect girl.) I suddenly spiraled into a deep mode of depression, self-doubt, shame, pain, and embarrassment. I turned to drinking very heavily while taking antidepressants. I withdrew socially and emotionally from friends and family. I quickly went from being outgoing, energetic, full of life and promise, physically fit, and self-motivated to becoming practically homeless, jobless, and nearly ready to throw in the towel and give up on life.

One night while asleep after an evening of heavy drinking and feeling sorry for myself, I heard a voice in my dream instructing me how to end it all—how to end my life. It was a voice, spirit, or force that I could not identify. It clearly was *not* the voice of God! This voice rationalized that I would be better off dead and not putting myself or my family through this anymore. It even explained the method I should take to commit suicide, which was to overdose on pills washed down with the bottle of Paul Mason brandy that was a fixture on my nightstand during that time.

Beginning to panic, I realized that this was no ordinary dream. I tried to wake myself but could not. I began to struggle but could not move. I physically felt a force pulling me down as if there were multiple hands on every side of me. Fearing the worst and becoming very afraid, I only knew to say, "In the name of Jesus! In the name of Jesus!" I can't remember how many times I said this. All I know is that I did not stop. The more I called on Jesus, the less pressure I felt from this eerie and evil force holding me down. This experience seemed to last all night long, although now that I look back at that moment, it probably only lasted a matter of minutes. When I woke up in the morning, I was in tears. I was shaken as if in shock. I looked out my third-floor apartment window on East 146th Street and Kinsman in Cleveland. It was summertime. I looked to the ground and toward both ends of the street as far as I could see. I saw that I was okay and that I apparently had been dreaming. What I saw most of all as I looked outside was what would be the title of the song I wrote in minutes: "What God Has Done."

I gazed at the sky and the grass. I heard birds chirping and felt the morning breeze and the sun—sights I had seen count-less times before, but this morning would be different. My keyboard and headphones were right by my bed, along with a notepad and pen that I kept handy for the sole purpose of songwriting. It was literally within a matter of minutes that I wrote the music and the lyrics to a song I have no doubt was given to me by God Himself. My life soon began to take a positive turn as I got myself together, put my trust in God, and began on a road to recovery to put my life back on track. I've shared this testimony with many people over the years, but there are those who, I am sure, have no idea that I was ever in a place that could have very easily been a place of no return, meaning taking my own life. I remember someone asking me if I was sure I wanted to share such details about my experience and my testimony, thinking that they were too personal and may come back to haunt or hurt me profession-ally or even politically as I have had aspirations to seek elected office one day. I was willing then, and I still am today, to ac-cept that risk if there indeed is one.

My only response is: what if my testimony and my trans-formative dream that night help to uplift, positively impact, or touch someone who may be at a low point of giving up as I was? For this reason, if one person is reached, delivered, and places his or her faith in God as a result then sharing my ordeal is well worth it.

"What God Has Done" © 1997

Have you ever stopped to notice there's a lot going on out there?

From the grass that's on the ground that no one puts down to the clouds up in the air?

You ever seen a tree wake up in the spring, bear fruit by summertime?

The sun is still going, stars still showing, and the moon still finds the night.

What I've seen, I can't explain; I just know from where it comes.

It's like the sky that's over me; it's just a joy each day to see What God has done.

You ever seen it rain, no two drops the same; where do rainbows go?

Birds in the sky still love to fly, and the world the ocean holds.

You ever heard the wind, looked around, and then it's nowhere to be found?

Heard a baby cry, looked into his eyes, and a smile replaced a frown?

I might not know how this is, but I know where it's from.

It's like the clouds that follow me; it's just a joy each day to see What God has done.

I often wonder which hand holds all the answers

And from which hand He spreads His amazing grace.
I hope to see His face to thank Him for His Son.
And like the sky that's over me, it's just a joy each day to see
What God has done.

"My Idea"

There are not too many ways to frame or write a narrative to introduce this next song. I married at the young age of twenty-two, and it lasted seven years before ending in divorce. The marriage would have no doubt lasted longer had I truly understood what it meant to be married, respected the sanctity and sacredness of our vows, been more mature, and ultimately remained faithful. Knowing what I know now, I believe that God has to be at the center, core, helm, and foundation for a marriage to be successful, even throughout the courtship before there is a proposal. Especially in times like these, He has to be the centerpiece and the tie that binds.

"My Idea" was written for the marriage that would never be, because, nearly four years after my divorce, the wedding was postponed and ultimately did not take place. I sincerely meant the words to this as they were written from the bottom of my heart. The song, however, has since been requested and sung by others at a few weddings, although it was written for my own. This in itself gives me hope that the words still have meaning and have resonated with other couples. They were united in holy matrimony, and this song is forever a part of their special day. I will write another wedding song one day for me and my future bride. I know now what it really means in its fullness to love your wife as Christ loves the Church.

"My Idea" © **1997**
My idea of the perfect day
is one that starts and ends with you.
And my idea of the perfect place
is any room where there's room
to hold what's in our hearts.

My idea of the perfect night
is one that you will spend with me.
And my idea of the perfect time
is here and now, before this crowd,
as you become my wife.

My idea of the perfect girl, four corners of the world,
is you.
You and only you, there'll be nothing we can't do.
That's my idea, that's why I'm here
with the perfect girl you are.

My idea of the perfect house
is one that is blessed by God.
And my idea of the perfect child
is yours and mine, with your eyes,
wrapped inside our love.

My idea of love is you.
There'll be nothing we can't do.
That's my idea, that's why I'm here
with the perfect girl you are.

"I Will Never Let You Down"

In a world full of disappointments and uncertainties, it is assuring to know that our God will never let us down. He has been consistent since the beginning of time. We do not have to wonder from day to day, month to month, or year to year if the sun is going to rise in the East or set in the West. For certain, the air we breathe that fills our lungs without us doing anything to generate or earn it is supplied for us. If we had to think about and make happen all that takes place daily in order for our complex bodies to function…that is all we would do. We cannot count or conceive of all He does for us. He never lets us down.

The lyrics to this song acknowledge that everything may not always be perfect or rosy. There are rough and challenging times that we all face at one point or another. We may experience some situations that may challenge our faith or take us to the brink, where we feel we can go no further. Putting your trust, faith, and belief in our all-knowing, all-perfect, all-loving God, who never fails, is what will see you through, even when you may not know how you're going to make it. I've been through some very trying and difficult days, and I am sure you have too. To close my eyes and cry out to God in submission and praise, only to feel His presence and hear His voice say, "I'm right here," is comforting and sustaining in itself. To trust and believe that He has a master plan for our lives and is still in control even when all may seem lost is what inspired me to write "I Will Never Let You Down." It's a comfort to me. It wipes away tears and sometimes rocks me to sleep late at night just to know that we serve a God who, if we plant ourselves in Him, will never leave or forsake us. I might have been in a lonely or lowly place when I wrote this song. I needed to remind myself of His promise that no matter my burden, I just need to be still and know that He is God.

"I Will Never Let You Down" © 2005
Now there may come a time when high is your climb
When the road starts to wind, and the end you can't find.
And there may come a day when someone might say
Your dream is delayed.
Dream anyway.

If I can climb behind the universe and still call you by your name
I'll be there for you, I will see you through
As sure as I light the sun each day.

I will never let you down.
I will never let you fade away.
I'm right here, just plant your feet on solid ground.
Be still and know I'm God.
Watch it be okay, My precious child
If you just trust in Me,
I will never let you down.

And, yes, the winds may blow around the trees

Cause you to lean, just lean on Me.
That's when you know I'm still up there
And I'm in control and for you I still care.
If I can climb behind the universe and still call you by your name
I'll be there for you, I will see you through
As sure as I fill the seas with rain
I will never let you down.
I will never let you fade away.
I'm right here, just plant your feet on solid ground
Be still and know I'm God.
Watch it be okay, My precious child.
If you just trust in Me,
I will never let you down.

I'm still the same.
I'm the same God, nothing's changed.
If you just trust in Me,
I will never let you down.

"Now's the Time"

If you are remotely aware of, observant of, and in tune with what is going on around you, I am certain you are noticing significant signs of the times. Be it in your local community, around your state, nationally, or worldwide, there is clear evidence that we are experiencing a series of events of epic proportions like never before. As I alluded to in the introduction of this book, I am not a theologian or a professional or spiritual counselor, and I do not claim the gift of prophecy, so I will stop short of saying these are the last days. If you just pay close attention to recent history, study, follow, and believe what the Bible says about times like these and what to be aware of, it may be wise to have a sense of urgency about strengthening your relationship and walk with God, if you have not already. No man knows the hour of His return. That alone should heighten our awareness of what is taking place around us. It should clearly be enough of an indicator for us all to pause and ask ourselves if we would be ready if He came right now.

The lyrics to "Now's the Time" speaks to just that, even going so far as to suggest that the time is now more than ever. This song has evolved over the years. I believe it was in 1991, in my good friend Gary "Block" Whitted's home studio in Ashtabula, Ohio, when I wrote and recorded the music as a jazzy instrumental featuring Block on tenor sax. Different lyrics have been written to the melody over the years, including a graduation theme performed at my younger sister's and late brother's (they were twins) high school graduation, as well as a love song titled "What's It Gonna Take?" Those lyrics were written by a songwriting partner I had in the mid-'90s named Tanea Woodbury. It was in 1997, during the same time I was faced with a spiritual crossroad in my life and was led to write "What God Has Done," that the lyrics to "Now's the Time" came to me. I was inspired to convey a message of how the world is constantly changing day by day and in many ways not for the better. Seek God as the answer and follow Him.

"Now's the Time" © 1997
If ever there was a time to look at the world around you
And look at the things that go on, it doesn't mean you have to give up.
I know there's still love, if only from above.
Because God is love.

If ever there was a season, if ever there was a reason
To make up your mind to stand tall and do all you can to carry on
It won't be long because help is on the way
Any day now.
Now's the time to give Him your life
Before this world gets any colder
Think it over
Now's the time, more than ever,
To give Him your life, to follow Him.
Now's the time to come together

To love, to help somebody reach the highest prize.

If ever there was a place for, if ever there was a day for,
A place and a day to step forth and claim all the joy in store
for you
Can you afford to wait any longer?
Before this song is over, think it over, turn your life over.

Now's the time, more than ever,
To give Him your life, to follow Him.
Now's the time to come together
To love, to help somebody reach the highest prize.

"To Be Touched by God Himself"

As I look back at 1992, I know it as a year in which my family and I suffered a great loss with the sudden passing of my younger brother, Lil Clint, as well as my grandfather just two months later after a long illness. To lose loved ones that close together created a void and a sense of grief I cannot describe.

My grandfather and I had become very close during his illness. I provided him with a lot of personal care, which would lead to long conversations that we had neglected to have over the years. I can remember shaving his gray and white beard and just loving to hear him talk. He would reminisce about times gone by, especially his youth and upbringing in Arkansas in the mid-1920s and '30s. I was extremely enlightened as he would share and reflect on his memories and experiences of the Jim Crow south. Like with many family relationships, we had our ups and downs over the years, but nothing would come between us to negate the love, appreciation, and honor I had for him.

For a long time, music has been my way of expressing my personal feelings, emotions, and events. I reached deep into myself to find words to express my feelings for my aging and fading grandfather. "To Be Touched by God Himself" was my way of saying thank you to him and to God. Through it all, I thanked my grandfather for being the only father I would know and for loving, guiding, and protecting me the best way he knew how. Despite childhood moments that were confusing for me at times, he, as well as my late grandmother, laid a solid foundation for me that I still hold close and dear to this very day. I believe God Himself was in the midst of it all, camping His angels around me and lighting a steady pathway before me. I could have gone in many different directions, seeing how I came into this world. So this leads me to believe that because of who God placed in my life and the love by which I was surrounded, I was touched by God Himself.

In the final week of my grandfather's life, I hurried to write, record, and even sing this song. It was on a four-track tape deck in my friend Block's home studio in Ashtabula, Ohio. The recording session took place there after I drove about sixty miles from Cleveland one day after work. Once the song was completed and I had a cassette copy, I remember going the next day to the hospital where my grandfather was barely conscious or responsive; he was in no pain, but the nurses assured me he could hear. I placed the small cassette player on his bed, held his hand, and told him I had written a song that I wanted him to hear. With his eyes closed, I played the song and sang along with it. He lay there peacefully but did not respond. I said, "Daddy, did you like the song"? He could not speak, but I noticed that moisture had formed around his eyes. I then asked him to squeeze my hand if he knew what I was trying to say in the song, and he did. He squeezed my fingers with the strength he had and held on to them for a few seconds. This let me know that, through this song, he heard me say thank you for all he did for me and meant to my life. It was my final tribute to him. He went home to be with the Lord a few days later.

"To Be Touched by God Himself" © 1992

To be touched by God Himself
To be touched by God Himself
Is like seeing a storm blow over
And to never see that storm again
To be touched by God Himself
To be touched by God Himself
Is like wrapping a child warmly in a blanket
As he looks into your eyes and then smiles
Well, I was touched by God Himself
I was touched by God Himself
Because He provided a man who wrapped me in his blanket,
Which has kept me nice and warm until this day
There are times we must find the time to remind ourselves
That we are touched by God Himself
We are touched by God Himself
Because He lets us know
He'll be there for us forever
And one day we'll kneel down by His side
Where He dwells
And be touched by God Himself

"If I Knew"

Have you ever heard an old song on the radio, and it takes your mind back to the first time you heard it? You know, that song that you played and danced around the house to in your youth or teenage years? Or maybe the song that you loved during your college years or early twenties that you and your friends could listen to for hours and lose track of time because you were having so much fun? Possibly it's your favorite hymn or gospel song that uplifts you every time the choir sings it, or you find yourself humming it while driving, deep in thought, on the highway. Well, "If I Knew" is that song for me. It has yet to be played on the radio or be released, for that matter, but it embodies such emotions for me, not just as the songwriter but because of the frame of mind it puts me in whenever I play or hear it. When the first chords strike or even as I read the lyrics, it instantly takes me back to the summer of 1992, when my life, as well as my family, would change forever.

The passing of my younger brother, Clinton Hall Jr., then nineteen, was an enormous loss to us all. He was a twin, a loving son, grandson, nephew, and brother, and to everyone who came in contact with him, sunshine on a cloudy day. He was full of life, energy, joy, and compassion and had a smile a mile wide. When he put his #32 basketball jersey on, be it in high school or college, laced his tennis shoes, and stood with his six-foot-seven frame, he was the real deal on and off the court. We all deal with grief and face personal loss in different ways. For me, writing this song a few days after he went home to be with the Lord after a fatal car accident was how I began to cope with my brother's—and friend's—homegoing.

You see, I have to live with the fact that despite how close we were and all that we shared, especially as he began to grow into manhood, I did not get to tell him that we were actually brothers by birth. He knew and related to me as *Uncle* Bobby. We still had a closeness that lasted from childhood up to the very last day I saw him. Time did not allow me to share with him what I was beginning to share openly with others—that I was adopted, and we shared the same mother—which, I have absolutely no doubt, would have taken our closeness and relationship to another level. I actually had planned to tell him that year but was just waiting for what I would deem the "perfect moment" after choosing just the right words and setting. Knowing his personality and his sense of humor, he probably would have said, "Man, Bobby, you kiddin' me? For real?!" He had just that type of easygoing and gentle spirit. He was wise far beyond his nineteen years and was especially loved by children.

Earlier that summer, he had come by my townhouse, which was less than five minutes from where he lived. I was in my home recording studio, working on a song. I had just started recording the music when he came into the room, his usual smiling and energetic self, and said, "Hey, Bobby, what's up? What are you doing?" I told him I was working on a new song. As he came toward the keyboard while I was playing, he began to listen. He told me it sounded good. I thanked him and began recording the drum beat. He then smiled and said, "I like that! You gonna let me rap to it?" I laughed and said, "Sure, Clint, you can rap to it." In his playful voice, he said, "Cool" and then went to my kids' room to greet and play with them. They were three, five, and seven at the time.

The song he would hear while I was creating it, which had no title or words at the time, would eventually be the one I sang at his homegoing service. I wrote the lyrics "Something About Saying Goodbye" to it. It was impossible for him and I to know while I was creating the music what it would be the foundation for just a few months later. This is why "If I Knew" has so much meaning to me. A few months after completing the song, we were playing basketball in the church-yard, which was a neighborhood basketball court behind a church not far from where we lived. I was by no means on his all-star level of athleticism, skill, and finesse on the basketball court, but we found ourselves on the same team that sunny Wednesday afternoon in August. I believe our team won three or four games in a row if he had his way on the court, and he usually did. What will ring in my memory banks forever was the fast break I was leading after getting a rebound. He sprinted to the other side of the court and gave me the "alley oop" motion, which meant for me to throw the ball as close to the rim as possible, and then he would catch it and dunk it in the basket. I did my best, but the ball hit the rim and then bounced off. He looked at me, smiled, and said, "That's okay, Bobby. Next time!"

Sure enough, a few plays later, the same fast-break opportunity presented itself. It was almost the same, identical scenario. I dribbled to the basket on one side of the court with Clint angling from the other side while heading toward the basket. He gave me the "alley oop" sign again. Well, the rest was history. The timing was perfect. I threw the ball above the rim, and he jumped up to grab it and slammed it inside the rim. We high-fived each other and soon went on to win the game. I can see us now, talking after the game, saying how we would catch up with each other later. That would be the last time I would see the smiling face of my little brother. He had no idea that I was his big brother as he went home to be with the Lord three days later.

So, as you can imagine, "If I Knew" represents what its title suggests. Read the lyrics to the song and download the music at some point from the link provided. You will be able to experience through word and song a fraction of what I have felt since that day of wishing I'd stayed and laughed some more with him. This alone is why each day and moment we have with our loved ones and significant others is precious and priceless. I am certain there is someone you cherish fond memories of and if you knew that the last time you saw that person would be the final time you'd ever see him or her, you would have stayed to say, "I love you."

"If I Knew" © 1992
If I knew the day I saw your smile
I wouldn't see it for a while

If I knew that was the last we'd smile together
If I knew when you were out there
Spreading joy everywhere
If I knew that joy would not be there forever
If I knew when I saw your face
That warm and sunny day
What a friend I had, how we laughed and laughed
It's like if I only knew I'd stayed and laughed
Some more with you
Some say I shouldn't be sad
But thoughts like this just make me sad
If I knew
I would have stayed to tell you I love you
If I knew the things that I know now
All those things I'd turn around
Like we'd spend that evening hanging out together
And if I knew those days when we would fight,
Make up, then say goodnight
If I knew, those days I'd hold real tight forever
If I knew, all those memories I'd hold forever and a day
When I close my eyes, look up to the sky
It's like I can feel the joy you feel inside of me
Some say I shouldn't be sad
But thoughts like this just make me sad
If I knew, I would have stayed to tell you I love you
There are times when I can see you in the morning
When I can feel you in the midnight hour
Like you wouldn't tell me that you feel the same as I do?

You and I had a special thing
Now I miss the love and the joy you'd bring
I would have let you know, told you so sooner
Been by your side, just you and I
If I knew
All the words that I never could say
I'd bring to you in a special way
If I knew

"In My Mirror"

It was during an emotional, defining and confusing time when I wrote the lyrics to this song. I left college abruptly after two rather successful academic years at Ohio University after learning I was adopted. It became extremely difficult for me to concentrate at that point and I truly felt alone, angry and let down. That era was sort of an emotional whirl-wind for me as very little made sense or even mattered anymore. As I look back on that period of time, I probably should have entered therapy or received professional counseling as my thoughts ran rampant as a result of the million and one questions I had that produced little to no satisfying answers. Questions about my life, my identity, my destiny, my family history, who to trust, what to trust, who to believe in and what to believe in. It was a time in which everything I knew about myself as well as my family was either shattered or redefined which left me confused, saddened, depressed and feeling somewhat incomplete, insignificant and misled in the scheme of it all. Maybe this is why I am patient, understanding and mindful of what a lot of our youth are confronted with today as I work with a number of teenagers that face many challenges and heavy burdens.

There were days when all I could do to keep it together was look in the mirror and try to figure out my life and which way it was headed after my foundation had been shaken and uprooted. I tried the best I knew how in concealing my feelings, 'manning up' and moving on. This would not be an easy task. It's been over 30 years now and I admit I still have my occasional days when my thoughts and or emotions quietly resurface. I take those moments in stride and deal with them accordingly as thoughts, memories and emotions come and go. I've learned over the years as I've matured and grown in my faith to give the rest to God who never fails to strengthen me. I now attempt to channel those emotions constructively in ways that may be of some benefit, encouragement and inspiration to others.

However, trying to uphold a strong and manly image as a then 19 year old, I wrote "In My Mirror" as if it was about a young girl coming into the age of discovery as she tried to identify and cope with inner feelings, disappointment, self-esteem issues and insecurities. Expressing feelings that she kept mostly to herself as she was convinced that no one truly understood her or cared about her pain. The song would be recorded and performed in 1985 by a Cleveland female teen trio "Ingénue" on Time Traxx Records. Ironically unbeknownst to me, this would be the same record label in Cleveland where my cousin Sunny on my paternal side was affiliated who eventually would introduce me to the paternal side of my family which I never knew existed. The reality is, I wrote "In My Mirror" to express how I felt about myself at a time when music seemed to be the only voice I had. A few years later after the birth of my oldest daughter, I would rewrite the lyrics using the same melody, but title the song "Kyerra, my baby girl" as a dedication to my first born.

When each of us look in our mirrors, we see, feel and reflect upon different things. What is it that you see, feel and reflect upon when you glance into yours?

"In My Mirror" © 1985
In my mirror
I see a girl
That needs a world
To let her in
To let her inside
It gets cold and lonely sometimes

In my mirror
I see a girl
Hanging her head just like me
And I can see the reason why
Why she is
Trapped in my mirror
And though I can't hear her
I know she saying
I know just what you mean
I see you in my mirror
And I know just what you mean

Mirror, mirror on the wall
Keep watching me in case I fall
I'm so glad that you're there
To share with me
Because sometimes it feels
I want to run away

I see you in mirror
And I know just want you mean

"We're Still Family"

This song has a dear and personal meaning to me as well. I share it as a message to all families that once were close and now are not—a family that may have lost its way for reasons that may be complex, but there is still a strong and passionate desire for restoration, reunification, and loving relationships to be rekindled. Although I wrote this song some eighteen years ago, it is my fifteen-year-old son who makes this song resonate loudly within my spirit. Though I love him as dearly as any father could, we live thousands of miles apart and have fences between us to mend. I miss his laughter and his smile as he grows into a brilliant and handsome young man. I think about this song, written before he was born, as I think about us. He actually told me once that this was his favorite of all the songs he's heard me write or record. That makes this song even that much more special. To top it off, Lil Bob has an amazing voice, an incredible ear for music and a natural vocal talent that he has yet to even realize. Oh, to hear my son one day sing "We're Still Family"!

If you are faced with an unresolved family situation, it just may take someone to take the first step, and that some-one may just be you after reading this book or meditating on the words of this song. Ask God to help your family be a family again. He already knows the situation and has heard your cries. He may have already worked it out in your favor and is just waiting for you to surrender all and to lean on and depend on Him.

"We're Still Family" © 1997

Now I think a lot of things
And I've dreamt a lot of dreams
Since I was just a teen
And I've broke some rules
What about you?
Ever just closed your eyes
Feel like you're about to cry?
But thanks to the strength inside
You cannot get your dreams
Off your mind
Once had family
I thought I had everything
Fun in the summer breeze
Now it's so cold we hardly speak
One day in came the truth
Changed everything I knew
But still that don't matter to me
The last I checked
We're still family
And that's the way it's supposed to be
You might be this
I might be that
We might be mad
But we're still family.
We're still family
And that still means the world to me
You might be this
I might be that

We might be mad
But we're still family
My father, who led the way
My mother, with us she'd pray
My brother who passed away
If he were here to see this
What would he say?
"I can't believe my eyes."
Then he'd say, "Keep hope alive."
So blessed be the tie that binds
'Cause this doesn't have to be
We're a family
It just may take someone (like you)
To reach out and touch someone
Remind us of all the fun
We used to have underneath the summer sun
"I love you" is not hard to say
But I'm afraid we're gonna wait too late
Let go and let God
He gave us to us
To be a family
We're still family
You might be this
I might be that
We might be mad
But we're still family.

A Closing Message from My Heart to Yours

While you wait, get out the rake.

Do you know that feeling of final completion after you've put in a lot of hard work and dedication, and you've planned as best as you know how? Through tireless effort, you have executed to the highest level of your ability while ceaselessly praying for that breakthrough or answer to be revealed to you? You've claimed the successful outcome you have so diligently and faithfully pursued and sacrificed for, and now you are graciously anticipating the fruit of your labor and the heavens to open wide in your favor? What might you do in the meantime while you wait? Let me suggest to you that this is the time to pull out your rake and start raking.

I'm not talking about the rake for leaves or for gardening around the front or backyard but a rake to sort out, gather up, and pull together the debris from life's trials and travails, scattered and lingering debris from old wounds, hurts, pain, and disappointments that may hold back your progress as it clutters the pathway over which you are still stumbling. We have allowed some of this debris to follow and swirl around us like leaves on a windy fall day in Cleveland. It sometimes clouds our vision and decision making in moving forward. We wade through it as if it were not there until we see the path we left behind or the residue on us that others may see but which may be hidden from our line of sight.

I speak from personal experiences as some of the debris that finds its way to me shows itself in the form of old wounds, unresolved family matters, relationships that have gone by but are still in my rearview mirror, regrets over poor choices and decision making, or simply the knowledge that I might not have always been at my best. Left unaddressed, this debris can accumulate, become problematic, or present a stumbling block that halts your progress and holds you back from what or even who God really has in store for you.

Even if you experience seasons of success, this debris has a way of resurfacing and consuming you if you never address it, rake it up, and properly dispose of it or put it into proper perspective. You see your ship sailing in, what you've been longing for—be it personal, educational, or professional— and with that anticipation, there is great wisdom in making sure you take and make the time to sort out and begin to deal with areas that have piled up in your life. You need to rake it in, see the debris for what it is, sort it out, and give it to God, the Master Gardener.

This may be an arduous task or even an emotional process that you may want to avoid. It may even be painful, with no immediate fix or resolution. Thankfully, with God at your side and as your guide, as you stand on His shoulders, you can and will make it. With His protective and loving hands around you, you don't have to be plagued by this pile of debris that might have hindered or weighed you down for years.

If this debris has dirt, guilt, disappointment, shame, blame, dejection, or rejection associated with it, you will no longer have to ignore, dismiss, minimize, or rationalize it. Finally, you will be able to stop sweeping it under the porch or into someone else's yard as if you play no role in it and do not plan on addressing it. You will be able to stop going through life as if you are without blemish while highlighting the blemishes of others, which keeps you from dealing with the pile of debris in your own backyard. You can remove life's debris in a way that it will cease to be a distraction or barrier in how you approach what God has in store for you and what God has done for you.

At some point or another, we all have areas in our lives we never rake in and discard of appropriately in order to walk in our full potential and the fullness of God's plan, purpose, and preparation for our lives. So as you wait for what you have labored and prayed to God for, what a perfect time and opportunity it is to not only get your physical and spiritual house in order but your emotional yard as well. That back-yard of your life, full of scattered leaves and debris for various reasons, is still there. As you take personal inventory, don't delay or just hope that a strong gust of wind will blow away that pile of leaves in your life. Get out your rake, gather what has been troubling and hindering you for far too long. In submission to His holy Word and His perfect will, humbly place it into God's unchanging hands. God is able! Let me rephrase that…God is *more* than able to sustain, undergird and deliver you no matter how high the climb, how heavy the burden, or how scattered the leaves and debris in your life may be or appears to be. In all you do, follow Him, acknowledge Him, praise Him, worship Him, serve Him and honor Him for He is worthy! Don't just sit there. As you get ready for what God has in store and set aside just for you…Start raking!